DENNIS POTTER

Blue Remembered Hills
and Other Plays

faber and faber

LONDON BOSTON

First published in 1984 as *Waiting for the Boat* by Faber and Faber Limited
This edition published in 1996
by Faber and Faber Limited
3 Queen Square London WC1N 3AU

A CIP record for this book
is available from the British Library

ISBN 0-571-17906-1

4 6 8 10 9 7 5 3

Contents

BERNARD: We can pretend we're waiting for a boat.

JEAN: We can even go on one, if you like.

BERNARD: Ah. But you don't know what sort of boat I mean.

JEAN: What sort of boat, Bernard?

BERNARD: The one we're waiting for.

from *Cream in My Coffee*

'Some Sort of Preface . . .'

There is an undoubtedly neurotic and probably incurable delusion, sometimes felt to be a curse but equally or more often experienced as an attenuated form of grace, in which a person from his earliest years onward believes his life possesses an especial and yet almost furtively hidden Significance that is always just about to be 'revealed'. Those who share in this condition—they tend to be dissatisfied priests, snap-eyed bores, blocked writers, madmen and all Scottish television executives—do not necessarily awake at each cock-crow with such a weird imperative bubbling away half an inch from their eyelashes, but sooner or later during the next day or two they are sure to be made aware of their ludicrous plight.

As for myself, the neurosis does not (I think; I *hope*) compel me at any one moment to do anything other than what I am already doing. It is therefore sufficiently mild, or adequately enough under a properly contemptuous control, to keep me on the outside of both the pulpit and the cuckoo house. I have grown wry and patient in not-really-waiting for what is supposed to be an instantaneous revelation which I am of course sure (reasonably sure) will never come. The road to Damascus does not pass by my house.

I no longer expect the expected illumination to rush out at me with a breathlessly apologetic bump and clutter from around the next street corner, like an extremely busy angel with a shopping bag. Nor do I any longer sort of half glimpse the oddly nicotine-stained and broken forefinger of an alarmingly jocose God Almighty jabbing down at me from a galleon of windswept cumulus. And I do not now wiffle my nostrils at the fleeting scents of a passing clump of foliated metaphors with any anticipation of a voyage that goes other than backwards.

Thus, whatever the 'significance' (inverted commas convenient-ly shaping themselves as the arc of incredulous brows) of my life has been, or will be, has not so far been vouchsafed to me—
Vouchsafed?

11

Recollecting (and, of course, editing) this slightly tipsy sequence of thought, which took place a few days ago on the train to London, I feel now an obligation to myself and my working habits to tip in a few stage directions. (The best two of which are always 'a nod' and 'a wink'.) On this occasion, there is no question but that my wine-moistened lip deliberately lifted in a deliberately mannered imitation of a supposedly fractional disdain as I continued to stare out of the scudding, momentarily sightless window. I had just conceded that a man in his late forties who used such a word as 'vouchsafed'—even in the privacy of the portable squabble-box that teeters and swivels on top of his thickening neck—is obviously about to start whistling between his teeth without knowing he is doing it. Fortunately, there was nobody in the opposite seat, unless it were the momentary phantasm of my younger, more priggish and much more disdainful self: the creature who too often tries to pin me down to his rhetoric, his intensity, and his shame-riddled intolerances.

Autobiography is by far and away the most boot-lickingly brutish of all the literary arts, especially when it purports to wrestle with personal motive. And such an inherently dishonest category of mislabelled fiction can only be made worse by letting by antique evasions in the comforting guise of redundant verbs. Vouchsafed, for heaven's sake. Prithee, watch what the fuck you're doing. One of the reasons I choose to write 'drama' rather than prose fiction is precisely to avoid the question which has so damaged, or intellectually denuded, the contemporary novel: '*Who is saying this?*'

If ever I dare to write any part of my own life's story in any other way except through dialogue and the movements or silences in between—and, yes, I will do so, certainly I will, once the never-to-be-revealed S–s–significance of My Journey has been revealed to me—then I will strive to find the right sort of language for the form: as slippery as Lucozade on the back of the tongue; fawningly complicit; nobly shamefaced about the smaller blemishes and not too painfully silent (but silent all the same) about the major ones; and comically interlaced with that

12

necessary degree of irony which is the sole form of 'honesty' modern prose styles or conventions readily allow.

The effort would scarcely be worthwhile. I do not believe what writers say about themselves, except when they think they are not saying it about themselves. This is not necessarily because they have less probity than others—though experience of myself and those of my colleagues I can bear to meet for longer than two scotches and a handful of peanuts suggests this may well be the case—but because the masking of the Self is an essential part of the trade. Even, or especially, when 'using' the circumstances, pleasures and dilemmas of one's own life.

All this forthright evasion is supposed to be an access into a Preface that I was reluctant to write. The publishers who had approached me about issuing 'three or four' of my old television plays went on to spoil initial pleasure by insisting that the project could be feasible only if I were also to provide thousands of words of introduction, and none of my arguments could persuade them otherwise. I have always presumed that people do not care to *read* contemporary plays, let alone ones written specifically for television, and I am even more astonished that there should still be publishing houses unworldly enough to claim a potential readership for a writer's introduction to his own plays. This is not unlike the offer of two addled eggs for breakfast rather than just one.

'But what if—' I said to myself, and I hope not out loud, 'What if I were to use this chore to describe what I think I am trying to do when I have a pen in my hand? And why do I always feel disappointed when the particular piece is "finished"? And—'

Caution. Caution. Sitting here on the train, with a book and half a litre of red wine, I am aware of a letter in my pocket which I have turned into something mildly threatening.

Dear Mr Potter,
Encouraged by the popular and critical response to a series of major interviews by Anthony Clare, Professor of Psychiatry (it was broadcast last summer under the title *In*

13

the Psychiatrist's Chair on Radio Four), a second series is now being planned for this year, and I am writing in the hope that you might consider the possibility of taking part in it.

The basic objective of the series will be the same as before, i.e. to identify and, so far as is possible, clarify the most significant influences that have shaped the private and professional lives of the people in the series.

Apart from the fact that they are, in one way or another, known to the public, the only other common feature between them is that, voluntarily or by force of circumstance, they have adopted or adapted to different sets of cultural, religious or professional values from the ones with which they had set out in life.

In order to allow for judicious editing, the interviews will be recorded at much greater length than the final forty-minute duration of each of the seven programmes in the series. . . .

I believe in the National Health Service, so long as it is in private, so to speak. But the very idea of participating (as the patient, or is it the client?) in a judiciously edited programme called *In the Psychiatrist's Chair* fills me with even more distaste than the degree of grossness such a series quite justifiably provokes. Perhaps incorrectly, I imagined the soft lights, the comfortable chair, the reassuring voice, the absence of technical paraphernalia, the seduction drawn out of intellectual vanity and public attitudinizing. By the end of the first hour—all wary bits judiciously edited out—I would quite possibly be streaking past the vigilant guardians of whatever mild neurosis it is that makes a person believe (and behave) as though writing were the most important activity of all.

The train was hurtling non-stop to London, bisecting damp grey fields and leafless valleys, reviewing January's England with just enough semblance of the way in which the hurrying mind scans the soggier and even more mysterious landscapes of its own impulses. Perhaps it is impossible to compose neatly

14

consecutive thoughts on the rattlingly straight, fast track between Swindon and Paddington. Even allied activities were difficult, for I had already skeetered three or four times along the same loose paragraph in the clever book I was supposed to be reading. Amazing how quickly the brain atrophies after the age of—what? Ten years old.

I made my eyes perch once more upon the black spikes.

'Television manufactures people in its own technological image,' I read, yet again. 'Its characters are creatures who could exist only on television: they are residents of the box, whose faces are screens. A later chapter, commenting on television's detectives and private eyes, will contend that, because television is so two-dimensionally bland, favouring amiable anonymity, the only way it can ensure a character's individuality is to burden him with a tic, deface him with a quirk—Kojak's lollipop, Columbo's scruffy raincoat, Rockford's beaten-up trailer.'

The tone is as unmistakable as it is predictable. An academic taking the poodle of his prejudices for a little walk. Freshly burdened, now, with a tic, and defaced with a quirk, I acknowledged that there is very little written about television which does not eventually betray smirking condescension or a rather less culpable unease. I have conceded elsewhere—though with one fist dangling low for a counter-punch—that to trundle the adjectival noun *Television* in front of the noble old word *Playwright* is not entirely dissimilar to placing 'processed' right next to 'cheese'. Nevertheless, I felt the tiniest murmur of pain as I allowed my eyes to fly back to the carriage window, barely in time to glimpse a few beleagured ash trees showing their bones behind a sagging stretch of broken wire fencing.

Once upon a time—ah, now, this must be another voice from further back down the line—*Once upon a time a soldier came marching down the high road, one–two, one–two, with his knapsack on his back and his sword at his side, and on the way he met a witch. . . .*

But once upon a slightly later time, when already imperceptibly adjusted to the dangerous treachery that 'telling stories' was also used to mean 'telling lies', I too began to be instructed (if not in so many words) that Art had a capital initial in the shape of the gable of a house which had been carefully and tightly built to lock out the crass, the crude, the ignorant, and most of those who made noises in the street. The beginnings of an English education, in fact.

Clack–clack.

'The poet is the intense centre of the life of his age to which he stands in a relation than which none can be more vital.'

Clacketty–clack.

'He alone is capable of absorbing in himself the life that surrounds him and of flinging it abroad again amid planetary music. . . .'

Clack–clacketty–clack–clack.

'The age, though it bury itself fathoms deep in formulas and machinery, has need of these realities which alone give and sustain life—'

Clack–clack–clack!

The overblown aesthetic of Joyce's youthful, lark-rising Stephen of *Stephen Hero*—which I interrupt with the sounds of an older train than the one in which I am now presumed to be travelling—is surely one which, at some stealthy moment or other, glows and burns in the mind of any young person who sets out to be a 'writer'. At the very least it tempers his alienation with the semblance of a human warmth, and elevates his perhaps necessary but indisputably ignorant arrogance into a mimicry of the *forms* of humility.

I pulled the Joyce quotations out for a lecture I gave last summer in Dublin, the most depressing place I have ever been this side of Los Angeles, where the decay of the spirit is projected forward rather than, as in seedy Dublin, backward in time. But the ordeal (as it turned out) of giving an hour-long lecture in a circular hall where the microphones did not work properly, and to an audience with a high proportion of academics and 'visiting writers'—and I was the only one whose work had been almost wholly within television, which made me feel not unlike some deliberately more prosaic equivalent to 'the lankylooking galoot over there in the mackintosh' at poor

16

Dignum's funeral: 'Now who is that I'd like to know? Now, I'd give a trifle to know who he is. Always someone turns up you never dreamt of'—the ordeal reassured me that my taste for self-dramatization was still intact.

The need to give shape to the lecture certainly made me dredge up old attitudes and aspirations of the kind expressed in the quotations from *Stephen Hero*. Perhaps I never really believed in anything like that pristine vision of the duty or the importance of 'the poet'—a word which, in the kind of discourse quoted, is invariably used to stand in for all sorts of scribe, thereby increasing their status in much the same manner used by little birds in puffed-up courtship displays. But I *think* I did, and there are moments, which tend to get longer, when a diluted or adulterated version of it happily returns in what could be understood as affectionate mockery.

On the way, though (and this *is* relevant) there was a not altogether uncommon passage through murkier lands. The ash trees through the train window remind me of them. So does many an old play of mine—such as *Follow the Yellow Brick Road*, broadcast in the summer of 1972. I didn't actually see its first transmission, because I was in a bed at the London Hospital, unable to move much else besides my left arm and maybe my penis, in an occasional erection which imperiously seemed to take no account of my collapsed hands, caked and cracked skin and feverishly swollen joints.

Jack Black, the central character, is talking on the other side of an expanse of desk to an out-patient psychotherapist who has not yet made it to the sunnier slopes of Radio Four. Jack is a failed actor who can get work only in the television commercials, which, unlike the festering Play-for-Today sort of dramas which appear to have rejected him for what he does not doubt are totally conspiratorial reasons, are full of demonstrably happy families gambolling about in the golden buttercups. These twenty-second commercial inserts, as pure as the blue speckles in the detergent, remind him of the radiance of the religious sense of the world he had once glimpsed as a child—a theme from which I, too, can never wholly escape (see *Sufficient Carbohydrate*).

17

The doctor asks him if he still 'believes' in 'God', in that tone of voice where everything seems to be in quotation marks. Jack is at first silent, then says 'No,' and then shouts, and then—

> For years and years I hadn't thought about it, hadn't considered it. I just—assumed—somehow—that he—it—was—there, still there, still watching, still present—Then—then one morning, day-break, I—well, I'd been up all night. Couldn't think. Couldn't sleep. Couldn't sit. Couldn't stand. I was alone. I could see the light in a chink through the curtains. First light. Half past four in the morning and—Oh, birds. They were singing. Mad chatter of them. A dog was barking, somewhere across acres of concrete. Empty yearning. First light. First sounds of the day. New Every Morning. I thought—I stopped in the middle of the room—I thought, it's been *like this* since the world began. Light pushing back dark. Birds jabbering. New day starting. What for? What *for*? So—so I tried to—for the first time in years and years I—it seemed—(*In a rush*) I got down on my hands and knees and I closed my eyes and I put my hands together and I said to myself, I won't ask for anything, won't ask, *won't ask*, not even for—(*Stops.*) I'll just let *you* come. I'll just see if you are there, if you are still there—I'll wait. I'll wait for—(*Gets it out*)—*the word*. I waited. I waited and waited. I just wanted the word to drop into my mind. I was open for it. Ready for it—

The word that eventually came was 'slime'.

'What?' blinks the doctor, knowing that no properly functioning person can be allowed to see the world in this way.

> That was the word! Slime. That was the message I got. No God. On my knees with my eyes shut I got this one word or feeling or impression or—I don't know—but there it was, long slippery strands of it—slime—nothing else but slime. (*Chokes.*) And dirt and—stinking slime contaminating everything. All over my hands. All over my face. In my

18

mouth. In my eyes. (*Shuddering now, in revulsion, as the doctor tries to stop him*) I was kneeling in a s–a s–in a sewer—*yuk* —lumps of—lumps of—*yuk!*—swirling all over—all over every—yuk —*everything*—

Exit Jack, at speed, his dirtied hands attempting to stop his appalled mouth, but the vomit rising too quickly in his throat.

Naturally, no one who gasped out such things in such a manner in such a place would be capable of one modicum of the detachment, let alone the discipline, needed to write such a scene. Pain and nausea are already transmitted into something else when proffered to others in the upward loops and downward strokes of words on a page.

And yet I am half afraid to concede that the excess of disgust jerking out from Jack Black's mouth more closely represented what I felt about the cold or faithless world, and its suffocating materiality, or my cold and faithless self, than did the earlier claims of Joyce's bright-eyed, ear-cocked Stephen. *Follow the Yellow Brick Road* reads now, to me, like the memory of a thumb being pressed too hard down upon a tender ganglion of protesting nerves.

Writing is, of course, one of the more obvious if not always most immediate outcrops of the author's impulses, resentments and unadmitted, misunderstood, dammed-up aggressions and hunger. But it is essential to understand (at the risk of asserting something even more obvious) that writing is not a displaced form of personal therapy, and is at its worst the nearer it tries to come to that condition. I am not, therefore, about to launch into a quasi-autobiographical justification of my own works, except in the much narrower and much more alert sense which follows.

The plays in this small collection were written after the (for me) low point of *Follow the Yellow Brick Road*, the manuscript of which might well have been delivered up to the BBC Television Centre in Wood Lane with tell-tale stains of old vomit on its wide, white margins (coals to Newcastle, so to speak). Looking at them again, I can now see a release from the kinds of extremities which Jack is made to near-parody in the tensions of his despair. What is certain is that if I had continued in the Jack Black vein, I would long ago have ceased to write anything worthwhile at all. What is possible is that I have once again reached the point where my apparent fecundity (or, at least, diligence) has been stemmed or diverted.

Joe's Ark has the kind of plot which, in summary, sounds like a winning entry in a *New Statesman* Competition parodying gloomy pretension. A young girl lies dying of cancer in a small bedroom above a pet shop in a damp Welsh valley town. In the shop, her chapel-going, eye-rolling, rhetoric-given father talks with malignant hatred to his caged and penned birds and beasts. Somewhere else, touring tawdry drinking clubs, her blasphemous comedian of a brother tells dirty jokes to drunkenly unappreciative audiences. A paradisial bird occasionally squawks, usually at the wrong moment. And it rains outside, it rains a lot. Just the sort of BBC play, in short, which gives ITV executives a warm glow of instant gratitude and appreciation.

But even *this* amount of mordant gloom, and even these spasms of evident disgust, are beginning to be used in a different way than in *Follow the Yellow Brick Road*. The resolution makes more than a wry nod at possibilities which can comprehend pain, or disgust, or the implacable presence of death itself. The viewer was not left with the thought that the only possible sacrament these characters could possibly celebrate was one which involves standing together on the nearest intersection of the dirtiest possible thoroughfare in order, collectively, to be physically sick. I won't dare to say that I wanted to send people to bed feeling *happy*, nor did I stray the advancing hand of dear old *death*, but the discerning critics (all three and a half of them) perhaps noticed a small hint or two here and there of a levity not wholly created out of scorn, or (if that is going too far) a momentary but descending modulation in what had otherwise been one long scream.

The facetiousness with which I describe my own labours is not, of course, because I do not take myself seriously. Alas, I do: indeed, I do. With all due solemnity, and my hands as near

20

to my heart as skin and bone will allow, and even with the after-image of a straggle of bare ash trees still lingering on my retina, I lay claim to be (at times, at *times*) an extremely amusing writer. The question is, therefore, whether the comedy and the so-called revulsion (once kindly described as 'Potter's celebrated disgust') proceed from one and the same, or from strictly opposing, sources. I can well imagine that the question is of considerably less importance to others than it is to me, but virtually the sole interest that I really have in this Preface (to three of what I would have liked to have regarded as 'trans-itional' works) is in addressing myself to the ways I think I see or feel the world *when I am writing*. The italics are necessary, because the rest of the time is my business, and directly concerns only those who are intimately connected to or inti-mately separated from me.

There are writers who have didactic intent, and there are some, I presume, who work out everything before they sit down to put the words in order. For me, and certainly many others, writing—however hard it can sometimes be—is more like pulling and pulling and pulling on a string that already has its weights attached, or dipping a thimble again and again into a pool that was already there. The effort, the curiosity, the surprise or the anxiety are each strong enough so to fill the mind that there is no room for 'thought'.

'Thought' of that kind—one's attitudes to life, to society, to politics, religion, and all that is not new under the sun—seems to take place before and after and around the act of writing, but not during it. I do not mean that one is a mindless automaton when crossing the t, dotting the i, or curling the comma: what, you say, will she say *now*? Why did he do *that*? He doesn't mean this, does he? No, they wouldn't look at each other, surely? Well, not with their eyes, anyway—and so on, and so on. Questions, musings, doubts—very concentrated thoughts, in their way—occupy a writer every moment that he or she is writing. A speech has to be torn up, a scene expanded, a silence explained. The mind feels very busy, and yet also oddly passive, almost as though *waiting*. . . .

21

Waiting for what, though?

Telling stories is one of the most valuable means we have for finding out about the world, but in order to tell a story properly you need to have made the effort to try to understand the shape of your own life. My first two published works—which were not 'fiction'—appeared to be heavy with genuine thought, but in reality they were weighed down with political and sociological cant, shuffling through cards marked 'class' or 'England' or 'alienation' with the ardently youthful skill of a tyro fresh out of Oxford who could pronounce upon the condition of his culture and his nation without knowing much of any real significance about himself. But this, in only marginally differing degrees, is not only a common experience: it is the way the world constantly diagnoses, and thus mistreats, itself.

What you are waiting for is your own voice, even though drama of any kind is made up of what purports to be, and what occasionally really is, other people's voices. But your own 'voice', the one you have to delve as deeply as possible into yourself to find and attend to, can too easily be reduced to the subdued babble of second-order memories (nostalgia), received opinions (prejudices), dismay, or resentment, or a kind of insistent, hypnogogic whispering which takes up so much space between the bones of your head that you delude yourself into believing that you are actively and seriously *addressing* yourself. Philip Larkin asks how the old ones can stand it: why do they not scream? I would rather ask the question of the young—but with the added overtones of envy, instead of fear.

The worst thing about television, perhaps, is the way that so many aspects of its administration, its technology, its expensiveness and its method of distribution conspire together (rarely consciously, of course, and yet seldom with genuine innocence) to diminish or threaten or drown out or even stop the mouth of that 'individual voice' which all even half-way creative writing must aspire to articulate. Those of us who have tried to pitch our tents within what is called the Mass Media are by now so used to trying to 'talk' and write above or through the jangle and the rattle that too much of the time we do not even notice it.

22

It has set up permanent camp inside our own heads, instead of the other way around.

But I must not exaggerate, at least not about what it is now like to write for television. The condition of the writer in the mass media is, after all, only a more extreme, or more exposed and compromised, form of the condition and the dilemma of *all* writers in the modern world.

I am not a Marxist, and I am not especially paranoid, but it is surely salutary to reflect that in, or on the brink of, what is laughably called the Information Society, we commonly feel that we *actually* know less and less about the nature of our society and the what, the where, the who, and even the how of its processes and powers. In the theoretical multiplicity of choices which technology is opening up for us, there settles (and squats) the apparently odd and indisputably frustrating counter-experience that somehow or other the choices we want to make—or, worse, the choices we want to strive to make—are narrower, emptier, less tangible, less substantial than they 'used to be' or, at least, than they need be.

We too often doubt our ability, if not our right, to control and so to limit the power of 'state' and 'corporate' overlapping, ever-meshing fiefdoms—and we endure, with an almost perceptible shrug, an unprecedented variety of social changes. These changes, too amorphous to be described as 'events', seem to arrive and then to engulf us without our consent, or despite our opposition or—the most debilitating thing of all—without our knowledge, and hence almost totally outside what we had taken to be our frames of reference.

Words themselves (as the last paragraph shows!), the very material of our discourse, increasingly take on masks or disguises. Beware, then, when I tell you that the exceptionally slippery word I now want to call into use is the dear old, mouth-frothingly pleasurable one of (oh, dear) *Colonization*. A porous enough concept to use to get at my sense of what it is *like* to be a writer in television and film, and even, at the furthest point of its elasticity, what it is often like as a citizen in the contemporary world. In short, I am asking you to grasp, and

23

then, if you please, swallow down whole (for the moment) the admittedly half-baked thought that you and me, both, are living and trying to express ourselves in a society which is ruled by an occupying Power.

I am not a member of the Social Democratic Party, but I do believe in recycling old material. It was my slightly perverse pleasure to elaborate on this thought—that of feeling as though we are 'ruled' by an 'occupying power'—in the lecture I gave last year in Dublin. 'Let me say at once', I said at once, 'that I am aware of the long and painful and continuing reverberations such a concept has in the mouth of an Englishman speaking in wounded Ireland.' Obviously I wanted them to stand on their chairs, not throw them at me.

The so-called 'occupying power' I am here stumbling to sort of define is not on the surface a malevolent one, not a tyrannical one, not even one with soldiers and policemen, nor one that knocks on the door in the middle of the night. But it *is*, or tries to be, ever present, and it is alien to whatever is individual, imaginative, and independent. And its effect—one might even say its purpose—is to push us, each one of us, towards an impotent acceptance: the entropy of a culture under alien rule, or the condition of a people only half conscious of their 'subjection'.

A condition that, enticingly or sufficiently adorned in ribbon and tinsel and pretty shells all in a row, might well be sold to us as something preferable to any sort of moral and spiritual struggle. The propaganda, so to speak, of the Occupying Power.

The trouble is, we cannot identify this Power. I am using it simply as a metaphor. Politics lives in cliché, whereas it should remake connections with analogy.

We most of us most of the time dwell within the human-made. A megaconstruct that has grown and grown until now it is so dauntingly huge, so insistently omnipresent, that it can be reduced to the proportions of 'understanding' only by attending to the creepy model of a spiral that is also a maze. Inside, we run and scamper, we ascend or descend, or stand stock still in twitchy bewilderment, according to a system of rewards and punishments so detailed as to seem arbitrary—and, therefore, beyond either prediction or control.

Somebody built it: but it doesn't feel as though it was us.

Once upon a time, unless it was a fairy-tale, once upon a time, and until quite recently, the human-made was more like a shell which we could leave and return to, and its horizon was within our view, our ken. It needed no simpler model than the streets of the city: real streets in the real city. We could walk along them, and, eventually, walk out of them, and shut the door on them.

But now the streets of the city have electronically (and commercially and bureaucratically) extended themselves into every nook and cranny. The salesman and the bureaucrat don't just sit on the doorstep, they come right inside. Sugared and syncopated solicitations come at one frontways, backways, sideways—and not always in so brusquely simple or comprehensive a form, alas, as the advertisement on many of the benches on the streets of Los Angeles: Grauman's Mortuaries—One Call Takes Care Of All Your Needs. 'I'll have you know we're all shareholders in this company!'

There are those in the world who more quickly, more urgently, and with infinitely greater danger to themselves, understand that 'words' have to be wrested away from the occupying powers. The *samizdat* covertly circulating from hand to hand amongst a relatively few dissidents (and heroes) in the Soviet Union is not a safety valve for intellectuals to let off their extra quantities of steam, but a breathing hole punched into an oppressive carapace. A tiny puncture through which air, *life*, percolates even to those who claim not to want it. There, where once noble words have been purloined and turned into their diametric opposite, where even pity itself is stifled in a Red Flag, there the *paralysis* is manifest and apparently inescapable. There, it is obvious that the true artist is the dissident: the one who will not serve.

And what did Solzhenitsyn's bleak gaze discover when he came *here*?

We in the West do not suffer the kind or the degree of the

pressure endured by those who seek to use real words for honest ends in the Soviet Union and all of its realms. Rather, the problem for most writers here is virtually at the opposite pole: indifference, and all its casual injuries. But good fiction, good poetry, good drama can still surprise and occasionally astonish us—though less and less often, and out of what seems to be a shrinking territory, and with what is a distinctly odd combination of increased self-consciousness and diminished ambition.

It is no news that there is a contemptuous, hard-eyed hatred of humanistic culture all around us. This hatred is both commercial and ideological, and comes from both the Right and the Left. Worse, though, it so often appears to emanate from within what I have to call 'Art' itself. In the long, grey, ebb tide of so-named Post-Modernism, pseudo-totalitarian, illiberal, and dehumanizing theories and practices lie on top of the cold waters like a huge and especially filthy oil slick. The birds can no longer beat their wings. We do not shoot the albatross, we slowly poison it, and clog its feathers.

Again, the word Paralysis insists upon forming itself, even as I pretend that I am looking out upon a winter landscape from a moving window. Again, there comes that obscure, ridiculous, yet persistently inhibiting power. *In the Psychiatrist's Chair?* Edited? No thank you! For there, at apparent ease, I would no doubt make things worse for myself by pointing out, with amused scorn rather than angry venom, that too many of those who should be or seem to be guerrillas against this admittedly mythical 'occupying power'—and who sometimes have the gall to announce that that is what they are—turn out in reality to be its covert allies in the destruction of humanism.

The overwhelming thrust of contemporary critical ideologies, whether Marxist or Structuralist, whether in the fractured syntax of the semiologists or the matted woof and warp of intertextuality *et al.*, is consistently away from the singular or the individual and in lumbering, flat-footed, tongue-tied motion towards the universal and the systematic. The academic critic reigns, intimidatingly: so much so that the old, old question of the relationship between 'the artist' and 'society' has in reality been suborned into a relationship between the artist and the academics. Poets make their bread in the universities, and then they break it there too.

Fortunately, or otherwise, the unregarded writer in the mass media does not have to work within such an atmosphere. He does not have to deal with these academic issues face on, so to speak. I am tempted to say that some of my colleagues think ,semiology is a sort of milk pudding, but that would be either condescension or wishful thinking. We may and probably do have the same urge towards respectability and intellectual acceptance, but deep down we do not really expect it—and if (oh, if) we are honest about what we are doing (and sometimes doing much more effectively than the traditional forms allow), we do not really *want* it.

But if what used to be called High Culture remains blessedly and usefully sniffy about television and—unlike in France—film, leaving the television playwright or the screenwriter as free of the ideologue's and high critic's throat grip as SF or thriller writers used to be, then those who have fallen upon or who have deliberately chosen these lower slopes and neglected screes are in consequence all the more exposed to those forces or processes in our culture which must, in the last analysis, provide the bacillus that shapes the theories, anxieties, neuroses and practices of High Art or Higher Criticism.

Television is the paradigm of the 'occupying power'. It is a universal and continuous process, universally and continuously manipulated, and yet it does not *actually* have a universal and continuous manipulator. There is not much need to go to the trouble of concocting yet another batch of conspiracy theories about who owns or controls it—would that the Occupying Power could so easily be identifiable, or the entropy so easily diagnosable and treatable. Indeed, I begin to weary of my own metaphor, although I suspect that if I could keep it going by substituting 'occupying power' for 'the establishment' in most of the stale slabs of would-be passionate rhetoric where the latter term usually sprinkles the prose, then (such being the prevailing mood of paranoia: a symptom of powerlessness and bewilderment)

I would probably make a small fortune as a pop sociologist with a new 'idea' to market.

No. Television, the manipulated medium, can only be misunderstood by any such neat venoms. It was once called, in all innocence, a 'window on the world', and there is still that about it, too. Where else but in the twinkling corner of my living room can I safely see a giraffe copulate or Mrs Thatcher deliver up a Christian prayer to journalists in the street?

Windows have frames, and they look in as well as out. But on the television screen it is most often when the set is switched off that it actually picks up a direct or true reflection of its viewers, subdued into a glimmer on its dull grey tube.

Occasionally, in the lobby of a big hotel, or high up on a building at a junction of important streets, or just below ceiling level in the corner of a large store, you can catch one of its cousins or appendages looking at you. And looking *at* you is but a short step away from looking *for* you. Where are you? *Where are you?* Ah! *There* you are! Behave yourself. Behave, behave.

The culture, our culture, is perpetually watching itself, or parts of itself, but the very technology which made such a thing possible implies that it cannot be watching itself straight, nor watching itself true. A technology, almost endlessly repeated, duplicated, extended, which necessarily overthrows many of the older crafts and trades, buckling the words that grew out of them, making quaint or redundant many working skills, and the words which go with them, and further distancing our labours from the finished products. These ramifications, which are verbal as well as physical, have inevitably separated many 'working people', at *every* level, from any quickening or immediate sense of the real value of what it is they do. Or, worse, from any satisfying or even comprehensible sense of its purpose.

I have often looked out of the train windows on the approaches to Paddington Station in London and at thickening dusk seen the tower blocks loom up above and beyond the suddenly widening mesh of rails. Nineteenth-century engineering which first created these tracks now overlooked by twentieth-century social engineering. And twentieth-century electronics, for at almost every porthole in the gloomy blocks, floor upon floor upon floor, the lilac flicker of the television set comes from deep within the rooms.

The people in these homes, stacked on top of each other in concreted layers, looking at the set in ones and twos or threes and more together, but not as a real audience in any older sense of the term, are often mostly watching the same thing (or the same sort of thing) at the same time. Many old communities, or, perhaps more accurately, many of the connections within these communities, have been broken apart, to be replaced with this flickering illusion of communality.

The advertisements which break up the programmes are neatly proficient little dramas which manage to mix nostalgia for what they themselves have helped to destroy, messages of almost evangelical comfort, and anxiety-inducing injunctions of the kind best expressed in the toe-tappingly tuneful brutality of that sweet old song 'Stay Young and Beautiful if you Want to be Loved'.

But look more closely at the programmes in which these commmmercials are embedded and even at much of the fare on BBC, where there are apparently no commercials at all, and you can still get the distinct impression that something is being *sold*. And this is not simply or only because the styles of the commercial makers and the programme makers leak into each other, as they do.

You don't know quite what it is that is being sold, but there are too many times, too many hints, when it doesn't seem all that different from the conglomerate of things being sold in the so-called 'natural breaks'. Too damned natural. And the attribution is made more elusive by the fact that programmes rarely show what people *do*, but usually what the merest surfaces of their *relationships* are: relationships that, again, are oddly aligned to the way one man or woman sells something to another.

Moreover, in the tension between the undoubted power of the imagery and the relative passivity—or, at least, domesticity—of its acceptance, what is transmitted is almost made to appear

The Way Life Is. The set is purporting to show us reality. By far the dominant mode in television is Naturalism: and so it is that most television ends up offering its viewers a means of orientating themselves towards the generally received notions of 'reality' —that is, the way things are, which is more or less the way things *have* to be. There is not much space left for what it is that 'Art' can do, and the word is mentioned within the dog kennels of this or that TV administration block as infrequently as decency allows, and always between the kind of inverted commas which are meant to show a sardonic expression.

When you have a book in your hands, or when sitting in a darkened theatre, you would be a bit of a fool to doubt that what you are experiencing is a 'made' piece of work, mediated through other sensibilities, given to you with a definite purpose, seeking from you another order of response. A response, an expectation, you are already disposed to give.

But one of the many dilemmas of the would-be 'serious' playwright working in the small strand of television which still permits such things (and that's not in many places outside Europe, and no place as well as in Britain) is, straight away, how to show that there *is* a frame in the picture when most of the surrounding material is busy showing the picture in the frame. How, in short, to insist that a play is a play is a play: or how to *dis*orientate the viewer while he or she, and your work, is smack in the middle of the orientating process which television perpetually uses. (I am deliberately exaggerating both the problem and the solution, of course, but that is a sometimes necessary privilege normally at the disposal of those who believe it is always better to argue than to shout but that the terms are not invariably mutually exclusive. So there!)

I suppose that I am saying, with some reluctance, that a 'television play' is always in danger of collapsing into the ceaseless flux that surrounds it. The prevailing, unexamined 'naturalism' of the medium as a whole, and the way the living-room set itself becomes just another sort of domestic appliance, continually works against that alert attention which any writer wants to evoke in his reader or his audience. And this problem

30

is over and above the normal and expected difficulties of
craftsmanship itself.

But isn't this—although in a more extreme form for the good
television writer, and against greater odds and in the teeth of
more powerful monsters and heathens—isn't this the condition,
or the dilemma, of the writer *in general* in our contemporary
world?

Isn't there the attempt on the part of many a modern novelist,
for example, to demonstrate way beyond any reasonable doubt
that his or her work is not, not, NOT composed out of the
apparent omnipotence of Naturalism, but is indeed a *work* which
points inwards to itself and to its processes? A twitchy anxiety to
make absolutely sure that the poor, befuddled reader does
indeed understand, my God yes, that *this is a novel he is reading*?

The writer today is more concerned with demonstrating that
he, the author, is not arbitrarily controlling the destiny of his
characters, nor overtly preoccupied with 'revealing' what these
characters feel and think. Unhappy with myth, wary of emotion,
harried by empty political terminologies, scornful of 'character',
eager, it seems, to refine, redefine and narrow down the material
until the works in question are about themselves, nothing else
but themselves. Affirmation, no. Consolation, certainly not.
There even used to be those who urged the writer to catch at
only what the eye sees, without characters, without feelings,
without emotions, thus dipping into and retaining part of the
world for the tiniest moment in its ceaseless flurry.

I cannot bear to rehearse here all those by now too familiar
arguments about why the great classical novel can 'no longer be
written', and how it is that its form and its assumptions and its
securities are *dead*. Most of the reasons can be heard above the
chink of the bone china when T. S. Eliot took afternoon tea with
Virginia Woolf, and told her—while pausing, I hope, to remove
a wayward crumb from his upper lip—that *Ulysses* had destroyed the whole of the nineteenth century.

We know full well that we live in the long shadows cast by the
old moral certainties which came out of one particular but
seemingly immutable clutch of views about our place and

significance in the world. The literary and graphic arts have all reacted with varying degrees of mental violence, despair or narcissism (extra, that is, to the normal posturing of their practitioners) to the strangely airless, weightless feeling which follows such acknowledgement. And the writer, tempted into selling himself as a 'personality', chat-show fodder, hype merchant, is in reality extremely unsure of his status, or, rather, his value within our new society. When many people daily 'see', sense, anticipate the multifold ways in which what is vital is being transformed into what is dead, they can easily (and often correctly) imagine that writers, too, are busily engaged in fostering the self-same decay.

Writers may still upon occasion pay lip service to the idea of a healthy common culture, but in their hearts most of them no longer believe in the possibilities. They sense that *that* old dream has been smashed into tumbling, cascading, falsely glistening smithereens—Pow! Zap!—by the increasing isolation or alienation or self-chewing narcissism of all of us, citizens at the mercy of those high technologies which take us further and further away from what we can grasp—hold—understand—and deal with.

And so it is that the writer, the artist, in the contemporary world so often commits the old treason against his fellows. He too readily, too frequently, bends the knee in the presence of that amorphous, all but indefinable, yet obviously existent aggregation of economic, social and political forces which I have, in a melodramatic metaphor, categorized as the Occupying Power: the apparently self-regulating, self-fuelled dynamic system which 'behaves' cybernetically.

But stop, I am depressing myself again! Flatulent and useless prose of this nature, which I suspect I am parodying rather too well for the good of my own soul, is what nowadays passes for critical intelligence. I suppose that I must be aping it either to deflect *or* to illustrate—no, *hint at*—the kinds of anger and frustration which have been causing me to think that I may well have written my last 'original' or (as they call it) one-shot, one-slot play for television. It is now nearly four years since I last handed one in, by far and away the longest such interval for nineteen years. So let me switch, and try once more to reclaim, in part, why it was that I so wanted to write for television. . . .

I was born into a coalminer's cottage in a stony village in what was then a relatively isolated Forest of Dean that heaves up in half-hidden layers of grey and green between two rivers on the assertively English side of the border with Wales. Brass bands, rugby football, nonconformist chapels with names like Zion and Salem, the sound of silicotic old men from the now closed mines spitting the dust out of their rattling chests. Secret places. Unknown caves. A mother who was a Londoner, bringing occasional uncles with outlandish Fulham or Hammersmith tongue, who did not say 'thee' and 'thou'. And when the teacher at the junior school left the room, which had windows too high for a child to look out of, she would say, 'Come out to the front, Dennis, and tell a story.' That was meant as a reward, or a compliment: it was, of course, a punishment.

See *Blue Remembered Hills.*

Through diligence, anxiety, accident and examination—and my eager complicity with those who made the chalk squeak on the blackboard—I eventually fetched up at Oxford. Willy-nilly being pulled away in a contradictory series of shame and scorn, pride and bewilderment, from the tight, warm mesh of sometimes stunted, often vivid alternative values into which I had been born and bred. The pale, timid and precocious child, not too badly bullied, remained clever, and added aggression to a secret and misplaced arrogance. Nearly all my classmates in the little school, long since abandoned as unfit for that use, were the sons and daughters of coalminers, as was my father, and nearly all of them are now working people. I don't know whether it was too obvious 'cleverness', examination salted, which ensured my early isolation, or whether, as I now dare to think but not inspect, something foul and terrible that happened to me when I was 10 years old, caught by an adult's appetite and abused out of innocence. But certainly, and with a kind of cunning shame, I grew for long into someone too wary, too cut off, too introspec-

33

tive, too reclusive, until, finally, as though out of the blue, or the black, too ill to function properly.

Perhaps we all live in a sort of exile from the lost land of our childhood. Not in the futile second-order emotion of mere nostalgia, nor with the lacerations of an even worse and even more futile remorse, and certainly with no heedless sentimentality. But simply, and impossibly, with the desire that we could stand where the earth once sang with magic, and look at ourselves as we are now. *Cream in My Coffee* tries to show, among other things, how dangerous or corrosive it can be not to have some sense of the shape of your own life, and how damaging to seek for what you are determined not to find.

How strange—the child would surely want to say if he could have seen ahead to what the man has become—how *strange* the things he has forgotten, how odd the things he thinks he needs. How *complicated* he seems to think the world is. How timid he is about whether or not he likes or dislikes something! And, oh, oh, what a lot of words. . . !

Yes. Too many.

Especially when the essence of what I originally (and calculatedly) wanted to claim is that, in the eye of a storm I could not then understand, I set out afresh to get my work on to television because I saw the need to do battle not only with the physical and maybe emotional handicaps of my own condition, but also with that wider 'paralysis' which is the enemy of all imagination. And to do battle, moreover, in, on and against the one medium where I could reach back into the fragmented remnants of the common culture which experience has taught me not to deny.

Only when cornered, I trust, do any of us want to burble our way through always inadequate and invariably inopportune Statements about the Purpose or Nature of our personal existence—and only a fool would volunteer them. I have, of course, been careful from the first sentence onwards of this rather wayward Preface to cloak or cloud or even at times to subvert any too direct or too heedless a disclosure of what I think I am doing as a writer. But although I have made little particular reference to the three plays or 'films' which follow, you do not need to work too hard to see that I have in reality been discussing them throughout.

Except in the opening and closing paragraphs, of course.

DENNIS POTTER
June 1983

Blue Remembered Hills

Blue Remembered Hills was first shown on BBC TV on 30 January 1979. The cast was as follows:

ANGELA	Helen Mirren
AUDREY	Janine Duvitski
PETER	Michael Elphick
DONALD DUCK	Colin Jeavons
WILLIE	Colin Welland
RAYMOND	John Bird
JOHN	Robin Ellis
Director	Brian Gibson
Producer	Kenith Trodd
Designer	Richard Henry

In this play, all the characters are children, allegedly speaking as children do, and the story is confined to the events of one summer afternoon in a wood, a field and a barn. The time is supposedly 'real' time, one incident after another without the imposition or intervention of memory in the form of flashback, or premonition in the guise of an interior thought as it might be experienced by any one of the characters. Compared with most of the plays I have written, therefore, it is by far the simplest in both form and content, for as well as taking place without hindrance, contrivance, diversion or any kind of secondary plot, the characters—being children—are not allowed eloquence, obvious introspection, rhetoric or even the useful consolations (and normal dramatic lie) of properly consecutive thought.

The only significant exception to ripple the surface of 'naturalism' (which, on the whole, I have almost always regarded as a stagnant pool, where the spawn never turns into tadpoles, let alone frogs and princes) is my prior decision to insist that the children be played by adults. I almost wrote 'grown-ups', but then realized I was talking about actors, who probably owe most of their skills to that devastatingly narcissistic 'Look at me!' which keeps the majority of them—including the octogenarians—still embroiled in an emotional adolescence.

I *do* have an aversion to child actors, poor little creatures, though I am fully aware that the dislike should more decently be addressed to their greedy, ambitious and appallingly neglectful guardians. It would indeed have been a dire prospect to have had seven of them in one go, but this understandable dread was not the reason I decided to dispense with the little monsters. I did not deliberately seek novelty or complication in the telling of a very simple tale, for in the trade which I follow so-called 'originality' is without question seen to be a curse and not a blessing, exactly as though a club foot were the consequence and not the cause of a limp.

Our culture has long since acknowledged that childhood is not transparent with innocence, and that its apparent simplicities are but the opacities of the very anxieties and aggressions which we occasionally seek to evade by means of a misplaced nostalgia for those 'blue remembered hills' of Housman's aching little verse. And yet although we do indeed know those things, we also (thank God) experience a countervailing grace when we actually look at children at play. The harsh north winds of anxiety and disappointment cannot quite erase the smudged chalk of a hopscotch square.

I did not want an indulgent 'Ah!' of softened retrospection to interfere with the sight of two little girls playing with a china doll, or four little boys deciding that, after all, there was nothing better than a box of matches for setting light to something. The fear of being mugged that I suddenly felt when stupidly walking at night in one of the many wrong parts of New York was almost exactly the same fear that I had felt four decades earlier about being waylaid by one particular bully in the high-hedged lanes which led away from my Forest of Dean primary school. And I did not want these, or any other, emotions to be distanced by the presence of young limbs, fresh eyes, and falsetto voices.

Another thing: children at play subtly alter what it is they do when under the gaze of adults, and since child actors are doubly under such censor, it seemed even more necessary to use the adult body not only as the magnifying glass but also, however paradoxically, as the seismograph which could more truthfully measure the quakes and tremors of childhood's emotions. Hemingway's characters may feel the earth move in their mutual orgasm, but a child can sense it spinning off its axis by the movement of a shadow on the wall.

Blue Remembered Hills

I. THE LONG SUMMER HOLIDAY, 1943. WEST COUNTRY

A 7-year-old boy, played by a mature adult, is walking along a path that meanders from some distant houses into a stretch of gorse and scrub common, and beyond that to a wood. At one side of the common is a pasture field with an old wooden barn in the middle of it. He is eating a large cooking apple.

At first sight, no doubt, he will appear to be an imbecilic adult rather than a normal child—his walk, his fidgets, his expressions and, above all, his mannerisms being modelled on the non-stop near-gymnastics of a 7-year-old, brought into compelling focus by the adult body rather than simply parodied or caricatured.

As he walks and dawdles and eats and screws up his face and tunelessly whistles he kicks an old cigarette packet, or throws a stick or a stone. But then he sees a long, thin puddle of muddy water in a cart or lorry track, and swerves deliberately to go splish–splosh through it, with great pleasure. Then, mouth full of apple, he starts to make aeroplane noises, extending his arms into wings, and breaking into a run.

This now swooping, zooming Spitfire is known to his friends as WILLIE.

WILLIE: Waaaaaaoom vrooooaaaaaaaaak! (*Imitates gunfire.*)
At–a–tat–tat–tat–tat–tat! Waaaaa–zzzzzzoooooooom!
At–a–tat–tat–tat–tat–tat!
(*Then* WILLIE, *at full flight, decides he has been shot down. The burning spitfire goes into a long death dive, 'wings' sloping, 'engine' howling.*)
Aaaaaaaaooooooooooooo. . . .
(WILLIE *staggers and crashes, with all due melodrama, sprawling on his back, finished. His run-and-dive has ended under the first of a few outriding trees, the gradual beginning of the wood. Four or five seconds of being dead are enough for* WILLIE. *He takes another bite from his huge apple, staring up into the sky.*)
Them be all dead. Dead, dead. Burnt to nothing.

41

(*A tuneless whistle, then a tuneless song.*)

(*Sings*) You are my Woodbine
  My only Woodbine
  You make me (*burp*) hap–py
  When skies are grey
  You'll never—know—dear . . .

(*His voice trails off. Comically, a pair of sturdy, short-trousered legs are descending from the tree above him. It is* PETER, *played by a fairly burly adult. A bit of a bully, but none too bright.* WILLIE's *response is a little wary.* PETER *swings out along the lowest branch.*)

PETER: Hatch open! Hatch open!

(*And he drops dramatically on the ground.*)

WILLIE: Hello, Peter.

PETER: What do you think of that, then, Willie? Good, weren't it?

WILLIE: What are you doing?

PETER: Parachute drop. What's it look like?

WILLIE: Yeh. Pretty good.

PETER: You got to bend at the knees, see. When you do hit the ground. That's Rule Number One, that is.

WILLIE: What happens if you don't?

PETER: You break your flaming ankles.

WILLIE: Cor! Bet that d'hurt!

PETER: That's the first thing you gotta learn my Uncle Arnold says. Him showed I. I be going to be a parachuter, see.

WILLIE: I be going to be a commando.

(PETER *has been looking avariciously at the apple.*)

PETER: Give us a bit of thik apple, Willie.

(WILLIE *tries to deflect his attention.*)

WILLIE: Your Uncle Arnold is a good parachuter.

PETER: Oy. Him is. Got medals and all. Hundreds and hundreds.

WILLIE: Do they keep their parachutes—bring 'um home, and that—?

PETER: 'Course they do!

(*He picks up a stone for no apparent reason, and hurls it away.*)
That's a good throw, that is. Near nigh half a bloody mile.

(*Sniff.*) Expect him'll bring I a parachute when him
d'come home.

WILLIE: (*Impressed*) Caw!

PETER: Two or dree if I d'want em. They be made of silk.

WILLIE: And summat else is—

(WILLIE *sniggers.* PETER *looks at him suspiciously.*)

PETER: Was mean?

WILLIE: Knickers is.

(*The two boys hoot and giggle. Then* PETER*'s expression changes.*)

PETER: I said give us a bit, didn't I?

WILLIE: (*Reluctant*) Him's a cooker, mind.

PETER: Wha—?

WILLIE: Cooking apple. And him yunt half sour. Honest.

PETER: Bist thou going to give I a bit or not?

(PETER *stands straddle-legged over* WILLIE, *so far only half
threatening.*)

WILLIE: You can have the core.

PETER: And you can have my fist! What do I want with the
flaming core, Willie?

WILLIE: Our Dad says it's the best part of the apple.

PETER: Your Dad is a loony, then.

WILLIE: (*Passionately*) Him yunt!

PETER: They oodn't even have him in the Army! What sort of
bloke is that?

WILLIE: (*Upset*) Shut thee chops!

PETER: Your Dad ent no blinking good for nothing at all.

WILLIE: You wait till I tell him! Him'll sort you out!

PETER: Yeh?

WILLIE: Yeh!

PETER: My Dad's got a stripe. (*Points to his arm.*) Him's in charge
of hundreds of men. Hundreds and hundreds.

(*The two boys look at each other, but* WILLIE *is almost in tears,
hugging the apple into his chest. Pause.* PETER *wipes his nose on the
sleeve of his jersey.*)

'Xpect him'll end up a general or summat. That's what our
Mam says—and her ought to know. Her cousin is a
sergeant!

43

(Suddenly, and defiantly, WILLIE *takes a bite out of the apple.*
PETER *scowls ferociously at him. Just as* WILLIE *is about to
swallow the bit of apple,* PETER *launches himself upon him with
shattering force.)*

WILLIE: *(Gasp)* Oof!

PETER: *(Shout)* You greedy devil!

WILLIE: *(Gasp)* Peter—no!

(He spits the bit of apple out of his mouth. PETER *subdues and pins
the struggling, gasping, choking* WILLIE *to the ground, planting his
knees hard on* WILLIE*'s chest.)*

PETER: Give in?

WILLIE: Get off!

PETER: I'll spit.

WILLIE: No! No—Pe–ter!

PETER: *(With immense satisfaction)* I will! I'll spit! Right in the
middle of your face!

(And he makes a huge frothy bubble of spit, ready to drop.)

WILLIE: Give in! Give in!

(PETER swallows his spit.)

PETER: Sure? You sure?

WILLIE: The apple's all dirty any road—thou's knocked it into
the dirt, loony.

PETER: Who's a loony?

WILLIE: You be.

(PETER tightens his grip, viciously.)

PETER: *Who* is? Who is? Who is?

WILLIE: Ow! Ow! Ow!

PETER: *(Grinding his teeth) Who*'s a loony? Eh?

WILLIE: *(Gasp)* I be—ow! Ow!

PETER: Who? Who's a loony? Who?

WILLIE: Me! *(Starts to cry.)* I be.

(Just to underline the point, PETER *spits on him anyway.)*

PETER: And doosn't thee forget it, you great babby!

(PETER releases his cruel grip, gets up, goes for the apple. WILLIE
wipes the spit from his face.)

WILLIE: *(Tearful)* There's *dirt* on thik apple.

(PETER picks it up, rubs it on his sleeve, bites into it.)

44

PETER: (*Mouth full*) Don't make no odds.

WILLIE: Germs!

PETER: What?

WILLIE: Horrible germs and things. You'll get the stomach ache, Peter. The dirt round here is really bad for you. Honest.

PETER: Pooh. Bit of dirt never hurt nobody.

WILLIE: (*Sensing a shadow of doubt*) You'll be rolling about in terrible a–gony. (*Sucks in his breath.*) There was a boy who died from eating a dirty apple. It was on the wireless. Honest. One bite, that's all. One bite and him was dead.

PETER: (*Alarmed, mouth still full*) Don't talk so soft!

(WILLIE, *who is brighter, sees revenge opening up before him.*)

WILLIE: That's why the RAF drops 'em over Germany. Dirty apples.

(PETER *has stopped chewing.*)

PETER: What for? What you on about?

WILLIE: (*With relish*) They do! So that Germans'll pick 'em up, wipe 'em on their German sleeves, eat 'em and then go home and *die*. In agony. (*Sniff.*) Good, ennit?

PETER: (*Alarmed*) Who told you that? If you're having I on, I'll—

WILLIE: (*Quickly*) It's true! Honest it is. Cross my heart and hope to die!

(PETER *looks at him, then spits out what is left in his mouth. But then has a thought.*)

PETER: (*Suspicious*) The apples'd smash to bits if they was dropped like that. They're too squishy.

WILLIE: That—that's why they fly very low. Dive-bombers. Aaaaaaa–splosh!–aaaaaa.

PETER: Who told you?

(WILLIE *draws in his breath, then releases a name of obvious significance.*)

WILLIE: Wallace Wilson did.

PETER: (*Impressed*) Wallace did?

WILLIE: And Wallace yunt cock of the class for nothing. Wallace d'know what him's on about, Wallace do.

(PETER *purses his lips, swivels on his heel, and hurls the remains of the apple away.*)

45

PETER: I don't want nern a rotten cooker, any road. Too sour for
I. (*Leers daringly at* WILLIE.) Give I the shits.
(WILLIE *giggles.*)

WILLIE: That was a good throw.

PETER: Best ever. I can throw an apple, mind!

WILLIE: Near nigh as good as Wallace Wilson's.

PETER: Better. I got the best throw in Standard One. And the
most deadliest.

WILLIE: You oodn't say that if Wallace was here. Him can hit a
butterfly out of the air.

PETER: Shut thee chops!

WILLIE: Anyway, we shall be in Standard Two when we d'goo
back.

PETER: Standard Two! Oy—that's right, Willie. We shall and
all! (*Wipes his nose on his sleeve again.*) Where is Wallace, I
wonder.

WILLIE: Down the quarry, I'll bet. Mooching about.

PETER: No. I been there. The Williams gang's there this
marnin'. They have got hold of an old tyre, the lucky
devils.

WILLIE: I'm not going there, then!

PETER: Got any fags?

WILLIE: There ent none to be had. Con't get hold of nern a one.

PETER: Ant your grancher left none on the mantelpiece?

WILLIE: No.

PETER: Nasty old devil.

WILLIE: And him do count 'em now. Told our Dad there was
two or dree gone, and I didn't half get a good hiding.
(PETER *sniggers, picks up another stone, and hurls it away. They
start to walk towards the wood—all over the place in their
movements.*)

2. DEEP IN THE WOODS
They rarely stay still, scarcely for a moment.

PETER: Can't you get hold of no matches?

WILLIE: What's the good of a match wi'out a fag?

PETER: Set fire to a gorse bush. Couldn't us?

WILLIE: (*Giggle*) Mrs Baker caught Wallace Wilson peeing on a gorse bush.

PETER: (*Delighted*) Her didn't, did her?

WILLIE: Her did! Last Saturday.

(*They start to double up with childish glee.*)

PETER: What—hoo! hoo!—what did—hee! hee!—what did Wallace say?

WILLIE: Him said—him said—

(*He has to stop so that they can laugh some more.*)

Him said as him thought the gorse was on fire and—and—

PETER: Hee hee ho ho ho!

WILLIE: (*Gasp.*)—and him was trying to put it out!

(*Overcome, they roll about in helpless laughter.*)

PETER: (*Eventually*) Wallace can pee the highest. I'll give him that.

WILLIE: Oh, that Wallace! Him have got a lot of belly!

PETER: And a punch like I-don't-know-what. A donkey.

(WILLIE *gives him a sly, sidelong look.*)

WILLIE: Made *your* tith rattle, didn't he Peter?

PETER: (*Stung*) Shut thee chops, Willie. I'm Number Two a'ter Wallace—and don't you forget it.

WILLIE: (*Sullen*) I gotta go.

PETER: Where to?

WILLIE: Oh—um—Donald Duck's.

PETER: (*Jeer*) What for?

WILLIE: (*Shrug*) Play football. P'raps. I'm easy.

PETER: Him ant got nern a ball or nothing! The sissy. Him's scared of everything.

WILLIE: Scared of his Mam, all right.

PETER: Her 'oodn't treat *I* like it!

WILLIE: I saw her hit'n with a shovel. Right round the yud.

PETER: Honest?

WILLIE: Cut his mouth and his ear an' all.

(*They fall silent. Then, as if to break a tension they cannot understand,* PETER *runs on ahead suddenly, and stoops over.*)

PETER: Come on!

(WILLIE *sprints, and vaults over him. They walk on.*)

47

WILLIE: I think I'll go and call on Donald Duck. We be going to collect empty jam jars.

PETER: That's a waste of time. There yunt none left. I bin all over. They be all bloody gone.

WILLIE: I dunno, mind. Donald got ninepence last week.

PETER: (*Scornful*) Ne–ver!

WILLIE: Him did! Him showed I! Seven two-pound jars—

PETER: That's only sevenpence, soggy yud!

WILLIE: And four pound jars. Ninepence, see.

PETER: Where did he get them?

WILLIE: (*Obviously evasive*) Dunno. Somewhere.

(PETER *glares at him, suspiciously.*)

PETER: Come on. Out with it.

WILLIE: (*Uncomfortable*) I bent supposed to say, be I?

(PETER *puts his fist to his mouth, threateningly.*)

PETER: You better had, Willie! You better tell me. Else!

WILLIE: Oh leave I alone willya!

PETER: I'll—ah—I'll let you have a look at my *Dandy*.

WILLIE: If I can get hold of two or dree big jam jars and take 'em back to the shop I can buy me own comic.

PETER: If.

WILLIE: I d'have the *Dandy* any road.

PETER: (*Put out*) *Beano* is better. How about the *Beano*—?

WILLIE: I'd rather have the *Dandy*. 'Sgot Desperate Dan.

(*But* PETER *is distracted.*)

PETER: (*Excited*) See that! See!

WILLIE: Wha?

(PETER *is already running into the trees.*)

3. THE CHASE

PETER: (*Shout*) A squirrel! A squirrel!

(*Warbling and hooting like Red Indians on the warpath the two 'boys' charge deeper into the woods after the squirrel. A wild, fast, breath-pumping chase, ending up beneath a huge, gnarled old oak, isolated a little from the other trees, at the side of a woodland path.*)

4. THE OLD OAK

WILLIE: (*Pant, pant*) Is him up there? Did you see him?
PETER: (*Gasp*) This is where him went all right. (*Pant*) By God,
    didn't him move!
WILLIE: Like lightning.
PETER: Him went up these tree like a don't-know-what.
WILLIE: We con't get'n, then. Him have beat us.
    (PETER *surveys the scene.*)
PETER: Him con't jump across to thik tree over there. 'S too far.
    Him's trapped, Willie. We've got him trapped, good and
    proper.
WILLIE: How we gonna get him down?
    (*They look at each other.*)
PETER: Frighten the bugger.
WILLIE: (*Enthusiastic*) Oy. Put the fear of God in him!
    (*They giggle with excitement.*)
PETER: Throw stones up into the branches. Knock him down!
    Eh?
WILLIE: Or climb up. Get a bit closer.
PETER: They got sharp tith, mind. Like little red-hot needles.
    And once they get hold of you they never let go, squirrels
    don't.
WILLIE: But we might be able to capture him. Live, I mean. Eh?
PETER: Nah! You can get a tanner just for his tail. That's what
    Wallace said they pay down at the police station. There's a
    lot I could do wi' a sixpence.
WILLIE: True nuff! Still—
    (*All the time they are circling round and round the tree, gathering
    stones, peering up into the branches. As they are doing this, two more
    'boys' appear through the trees. They are* JOHN *and, in cowboy hat
    and gun-belt,* RAYMOND.)
JOHN: What's up in thik tree, then?
WILLIE: How be, John. Hello, Raymond.
RAYMOND: (*Grin*) How b–be.
    (RAYMOND *is almost always grinning. But, alas, he also stutters.*)
PETER: We got us a squirrel, John.
JOHN: (*Delighted*) Have ya? Honest?

RAYMOND: (*Excited*) Wh–Where? Where?

> (*He pulls out his lead pistol.*)

WILLIE: Him's *trapped* up there. Good—ennit! We have really got
him!

JOHN: (*Peering up*) Ah, but how are you going to get him down?
You bent going to get him down. Him'll never come down
from there. You tell me how you are going to get him down.

> (*But* RAYMOND *has been working his face.*)

RAYMOND: P–P–Poor littool devil.

PETER: (*To* JOHN) Throw stones, o' course. Knock him down.
That'll do't.

JOHN: (*Sniff*) Be better to climb up. You tell me how you are
going to get him down.

WILLIE: Don't keep on.

PETER: (*Jeer*) Who's going to climb up there! Break your neck.
Aaaaaaa–crack! Just like that, loony!

JOHN: Wallace Wilson ood. Him ood goo up there. Like a shot.

RAYMOND: W–Why don't we l–l–lul–leave it al–lul–lone—?

PETER: Hark at him!

JOHN and WILLIE: (*Sing*) When the mum–moon shines
> On the cuc–cowshed—

> (RAYMOND'*s smile wavers. They peer up into the tree again.*)

WILLIE: I reckon we ought to catch him alive. Put him on show.
Be the start of a circus. No—it ood, though. Wouldn't it?

JOHN: (*The sceptic*) How do we know him's still up there? You tell
me that. I con't see nothing. Him ent up there.

PETER: That's where him is, all right. Look! See!

> (PETER *aims with his forefinger and makes a gun noise. This, in
> turn, triggers off the other three. Whooping and yelling and letting
> off 'gunfire' they hop and dance round and round the tree. Up, up, in
> the thick foliage—a swift glimpse of a squirrel.*)

5. THE OLD BARN. NEARBY. SAME TIME

*Wooden. Cobwebs at a broken window. A scatter of tools. A wheelbarrow.
An old feeding trough. A big pil• of hay. A cartwheel etc.—A great place
to play.*

Two 7-year-old girls, ANGELA, *pretty, with ringlet curls and blue ribbons, and* AUDREY, *who is plain, with cheap owl-like metal-framed glasses and short, straight hair, are 'playing house' with the splay-footed, timid, anaemic looking boy nicknamed* DONALD DUCK, *who has shoes or boots, but no socks. He also has nasty scabs round his mouth. An abused child.*

They have a battered squeaking old pram with a buckled wheel, which holds a chocolate-coloured china doll called 'Dinah'. Dinah, when tilted, closes her eyes and emits a plaintive little 'Ma–ma! Ma–ma!'

Pretty ANGELA—*who owns the doll—tilts and tilts Dinah, watched with an extremely aggressive expression by disgruntled* AUDREY.

ANGELA: (*As Dinah 'cries'*) Now, now, now. Go to sleep, Dinah. You naughty naughty *naughty* little babby.

AUDREY: Smack her one in the chops, Angela. That'll keep her quiet!

DONALD: No, no. You can't do that. No smacking. Not in my house.

ANGELA: (*To Dinah*) There, there, there. Mummy is with oo den.

DONALD: You can't hit a little babby, Audrey. You'd kill it.

AUDREY: What dost thee know about it, Donald Duck? You ant never had a babby. Smack her arse, Angela.

DONALD: I be supposed to be the Daddy here, byunt I? And—and—Don't call me Donald Duck.

ANGELA: No. Don't call him that, Aud. You *are* the Daddy, Donald. Coming home from work, aren't you?

DONALD: (*Smirk*) That's right. I be tired out and all, working on them sawmills. I cut me thumb off and all. (*Imitates saw.*) Zzzzzzzzz–chop! Ow! Ow! Bang goes me thumb.

ANGELA: Oh, dear. Poor, poor Donald. My poor husband.

DONALD: Ow! Ow! Ow! It don't half hurt. Blood all over the saw. Blood all over me. Blood everywhere. Blood. Blood!

ANGELA: Never mind. I'll put the kettle on. We'll have us a nice cup of tea.

DONALD: With four lots of sugar. Eh?

AUDREY: (*Aggressive*) Are *you* Mummy, then? Why should *you* be Mummy all the time?

ANGELA: 'Course I be. I got the babby, ant I? It chunt *your* doll, Audrey.

AUDREY: Who be *I*, then?

DONALD: Where's my bloody tea, Missis? Where's my tea, then? I want my cup of tea!

(DONALD *is stamping up and down in angry imitation of 'Authority'.*)

ANGELA: The kettle's just coming up to the boil, sweetie pie.

DONALD: (*With enormous deliberation*) I should bloody damn and bloody blast and bugger and bloody flaming bloody think so and all. Give us a kiss.

(*He hugs himself in glee, rocking slightly.*)

AUDREY: (*Insistent*) Who be I then? Eh? Tell me that!

ANGELA: Oh, Aud–rey!

AUDREY: I bent just going to do nothing and be nobody. It's not fair.

ANGELA: You can be my other daughter, Audrey. My naughty daughter.

AUDREY: (*Stamps foot.*) No. I'm not going to be that. No!

(DONALD *is coming out of his trance-like reverie.*)

DONALD: Aw come on, Aud. Doosn't spoil it.

AUDREY: (*Hotly*) *I'm* not spoiling it.

DONALD: Yes you are. You always do. Don't her, Angela?

(ANGELA *crosses her arms in mimicry of adult exasperation.*)

ANGELA: Who'd you want to be, Aud?

(AUDREY*'s eyes glint.*)

AUDREY: The Nurse. I wanna be the Nurse. With a little scissors.

DONALD: Oy—that's a good 'un. You can see to my finger. I mean, me thumb. When I've had my bit of tea.

AUDREY: What's wrong with your thumb?

DONALD: Cut the bugger off, ant I? Zzzzzzz. Aaaaaagh!

(ANGELA *tilts her nose in disapproval.*)

ANGELA: You want to stop swearing, Donald Duck.

DONALD: (*Pained*) Doosn't call I that, Angela! You promised!

AUDREY: Let me see thik thumb. I got some special stuff in my bag in my car. I'll stick'n back on.

(ANGELA *is looking at* DONALD. *Suddenly, as he shows* AUDREY *his thumb—*)

ANGELA: Quack! Quack! Quack!

(*Deeply upset,* DONALD *jerks his hand away from* AUDREY.)

DONALD: Angela! Don't do that!

AUDREY: Oh, dear. Oh, dear. I'll have to put some stingy stuff on that. It'll make you jump, mind.

(DONALD *is giving* ANGELA *anguished looks.*)

ANGELA: (*Responding*) He'll have to have his tea first, Nurse. He needs his hot cup of tea.

AUDREY: I can't wait around all day. You want to clean this place up, too. I can't wait.

ANGELA: No, and I'm not letting his tea get cold neither. I'm not slaving away here all day for him to come in at all hours and think his bit of tea have got to be ready and waiting. I'm sick to death of it, I can tell you.

AUDREY: Oo, Angie. That's our Mam, that is!

DONALD: (*Smirk*) Hurry up. I be off up to the *bloody* pub in half a tick. To get *bloody* drunk.

ANGELA: I shall wash thy mouth out with soap!

AUDREY: (*Pleased*) Shall us, Angela? Shall us?

DONALD: Nine or ten pints of scrumpy, that's what I want. I've lost a lot of blood.

(AUDREY *grabs his thumb.*)

ANGELA: You're not coming home stinking of drink at all hours and expect *me* to put up with it are you?

(AUDREY *sucks his thumb.*)

DONALD: (*Excited*) Shut thee mouth, 'ooman. Nag, nag, nag. I'm not going to put up with it, so there.

AUDREY: (*Spits.*) There. I've stopped the blood gushing out. You'll die in a minute, though. *Really* die, I mean.

DONALD: Brave, aren't I? I bent half bloody brave, mind!

(*A sudden shift from* ANGELA.)

ANGELA: Quack! Quack! Quack!

DONALD: Shut up!

AUDREY: Smack her one, Donald.

ANGELA: Yes, and if he hits me I shall tell his Mam. Her'll skin him alive, won't her, Donald Duck? Won't her? She hits you with the poker, don't she!

DONALD: Leave me alone. Leave me alone.

ANGELA: Quack! Quack! Quack!

DONALD: (*Scream*) Shut up! Shut up!

> (AUDREY *looks at* ANGELA. *Their eyes seem to flare. They join forces.*)

AUDREY: (*Venomously*) Quack! Quack! Quack!

> (*Horribly, the two girls round on him.*)

DONALD: (*Tearful*) Please don't. Please don't. Please.

AUDREY and ANGELA: Donald Duck! Donald Duck! Quack! Quack! Quack! Donald Duck! Quack! Quack!

> (*Jabbing their forefingers at him, they drive him towards the barn wall. He claps his hands to his ears to shut out their jeering taunts. In what looks, in adult form, almost like a psychotic frenzy, the two girls—and particularly* AUDREY—*tug and pull at his hair. He howls, totally submissive.*)

6. THE OLD OAK. SAME TIME

A grey blur as a stunned squirrel, hit by a stone, hurtles out of the tree, down on to the ground beneath.

> PETER, JOHN, WILLIE *and* RAYMOND *immediately close up around the animal, frenziedly kicking at it with their large, hob-nailed, toe-scuffed boots. As they kill the squirrel they giggle and grunt and gasp with shocked awe and excitement. The violent activity stops, abruptly. They stand off a bit, looking at each other guiltily. The wind shifts and sighs in the big old oak.*

A feeling of murder.

RAYMOND: (*Eventually*) Is—is him d–dud–dead?

PETER: Oy. 'Course him is. Deader than dead.

JOHN: (*Awed*) Him couldn't live through that.

> (*Pause.*)

RAYMOND: (*Bleakly*) D–Dud–Dead.

> (JOHN *shifts from foot to foot.*)

JOHN: They don't half sink their teeth in, mind. When they get the chance. We *had* to do it. (*Swallow.*) Didn't us?

WILLIE: We bent going to cut his tail off, be us?

> (*They look at each other, uncertain.*)

PETER: Anybody got a knife?

JOHN: Raymond have. A proper 'un.

PETER: Have ya, Ray?

RAYMOND: (*Proudly*) 'S army knife. C–c–c—
    (*But it takes too long.*)

JOHN: Commando. 'S commando knife.

RAYMOND: (*Finally*) —c–commando.

PETER: Let's see. Where did you get it?

JOHN: Him won't say.

PETER: Come on, let's have a look. Show us.

RAYMOND: (*Suddenly*) N–No!

PETER: What's the matter with *you*?

WILLIE: What's up Raymond?

    (RAYMOND *screws up his face.*)

RAYMOND: (*Half sob*) P–Pup–Poor little devil!

PETER: Don't be such a baby!

RAYMOND: We k–kuk–killed him— (*Sob.*)

    (*Obscurely ashamed,* PETER *gives* RAYMOND *a heavy shove.*)

JOHN: Hey! Leave him alone!

PETER: (*Snarl*) I'll knock his cowboy hat off for him.

JOHN: No you won't. Just you leave him alone.

PETER: Oh? Who says so?

JOHN: You heard!

PETER: Keep out of it. Keep your nose out of it.

JOHN: Flamin' bully.

PETER: You're asking for it, you are.

JOHN: Oh? And who's going to give it to me, then?

PETER: I will if thou doosn't watch it.

JOHN: Yeh?

PETER: Yeh!

JOHN: Yeh?

PETER: Yeh!

    (*They are toe to toe, but each is unsure enough of the other not to be too eager to put it to the test. Pause.*)

JOHN: (*None too confident*) Yeh?

PETER: Ah! Shut up!

    (*And he turns away.*)

WILLIE: Wish I had a knife. My Dad won't let me.

RAYMOND: Oh, them be v–vuv–very useful.

WILLIE: (*Sigh*) I could do with me a good sharp knife. By God I
could.

PETER: Wos want for'n, Raymond old pal? I be good with a
knife. (*Makes throwing gesture.*) Clunk!

RAYMOND: N–Nothing.

JOHN: Him daren't swap thik knife. All him d'do is clean it and
sharpen it and clean it and sharpen it.

WILLIE: Let's have a look, Ray. Come on.

RAYMOND: No!

JOHN: What's up?

PETER: Why not?

(RAYMOND *points to the dead squirrel.*)

RAYMOND: You'll c–cu–cut off his t–t–t—

(*But instead of getting the word out he bursts into tears. They all
look at the squirrel again. Pause.* WILLIE, *now, is also close to
tears.*)

WILLIE: I wish we—

PETER: Ah, shut up.

WILLIE: (*Upset*) No—I wish we hadn't—you know—

JOHN: And me.

PETER: They be *savage*, bent 'um?

JOHN: I don't fancy cutting off his tail, though. It's all gristle and
stuff, any road.

WILLIE: (*Sucks in breath.*) I bent touching him!

PETER: (*Disgusted*) Great babbies. I'll twist it off, then.

WILLIE: The blood won't half gush out, mind. All over you.

JOHN: Like when our dog got knocked down.

RAYMOND: P–Pup–Poor old R–Rover.

WILLIE: Nice dog, wasn't he?

JOHN: I'd rather get some jam jars, meself. 'Tent bad money
a'ter all, is it? Penny back on a two-pound jar.

RAYMOND: Let's l–lul–look for some. Eh?

PETER: There ent none to be had. They've all been found, what
there is. I've looked all over.

WILLIE: Donald Duck got hold of some.

JOHN: (*Interested*) Did he, Willie?

WILLIE: Him had a whole sackful yesterday. I saw 'em. (*Giggle*) Donald oodn't show I what was in the bag till I said I'd kick his head in.

JOHN: Little weed, ent he?

PETER: A cry baby.

JOHN: One punch and him'll give in. One punch that's all.

PETER: (*Flapping arms*) Quack! Quack! Quack!
    (*They all laugh.*)

WILLIE: Him have got hold of a box of matches an' all.

PETER: (*Very interested*) Have 'a?

JOHN: He goes through his Mam's handbag.

PETER: No wonder her d'knock him about.

RAYMOND: P–Pup–Poor D–Donald.

PETER: (*Jeer*) Him do ask for it! He set light to their coal shed, didn't he!

WILLIE: Only when his Mam shut him up in it, though.

JOHN: Our Mam says her's a bit of a thing.

PETER: How's mean?

JOHN: I dunno. Something to do with the sheets.

WILLIE: What?

JOHN: I dunno. Our Mam said them bed sheets could tell a pretty tale.

WILLIE: Perhaps her do wet the bed. Eh?
    (*Sniggers all round.*)

PETER: Let's go and find him. Donald Duck. And have a bit o' fun.

JOHN: Oy. And find out about them jam jars. Where do him get 'em?

PETER: Make him tell us.

JOHN: Oy!

PETER: (*Gleeful*) Give him a Chinese burn.

RAYMOND: That d–dud–do hurt, mind!
    (*They roar with laughter. But then, somehow, look at the dead squirrel and fall silent.*)

WILLIE: Him'll stink if we d'leave him there.

JOHN: Let's bury him.

PETER: Gettoff!

JOHN: No—a *proper* funeral. You know.

WILLIE: 'S good idea!

PETER: Don't be so soft.

JOHN: No—a *proper* funeral. You know. With a coffin and all.

(WILLIE *coughs elaborately.*)

PETER: What's up with thee?

WILLIE: Coughing. A proper coffin.

(*They all fall about, howling and hooting with laughter.*)

PETER: (*Gasp*) By gar, Willie. That's a good 'un!

(*Which provokes another burst of laughter.*)

7. THE BARN

'DONALD DUCK', *left alone, sits huddled up aginst the wall, in a foetal position, crying his eyes out. He grinds his fists into his eyes in despair. The hard, desolate crying stops, or subsides. And, slowly at first, he starts to rock. At the same time he begins a dull, monotone chant.*

DONALD: (*Rock*) Come–back–Dad–come–back–Dad–come–
back–Dad–come–back–Dad–come–back–Dad. . . .

(*The words die away as the rocking gets faster and faster, and he gets stiffer and stiffer until he is almost catatonic, his back thumping hard against the wall. Thump–thump–thump–thump. . . .*)

8. THE FIELD

The path from barn through the field towards the wood.

In the distance, ANGELA *and* AUDREY *pushing the pram along the path. Squeak–squeak–squeak goes the pram.*

We come closer to watch and listen.

AUDREY: . . . and her wouldn't tell, I, see. So I said, I said, Well
Betty, I said, I'm not speaking to you no more. You're not
my Best Friend no more, I said.

ANGELA: No, her's sly, Aud.

AUDREY: *You're* my Best Friend, Angela.

ANGELA: (*Smirk*) Yes.

(*Squeak–squeak–squeak.*)

AUDREY: (*With sidelong look*) Am I *your* Best Friend as well?

ANGELA: I'm Best Friend to lots and lots.

AUDREY: Oooh. Hark who's talking!

ANGELA: Oh, yes. Lots and lots. Especially the boys.

(AUDREY *works her mouth a bit, and glares.*)

AUDREY: Are you Wallace Wilson's best friend?

ANGELA: We be going to get married. With a ring and all.

AUDREY: Funny.

ANGELA: Wos mean?

AUDREY: I heard as him was going to marry Hilary Jones.

ANGELA: Her's too stuck up.

AUDREY: (*Smirk*) He don't half like her, though.

ANGELA: He can't. She's got a big nose.

(*Squeak–squeak–squeak.*)

AUDREY: Shall I bash her in for you?

ANGELA: Would you? Audrey—eh?

AUDREY: Ea–sy.

ANGELA: Bash her on the nose, then. Hit her on her great big fat conk!

AUDREY: I'll smack her in the mouth as well.

(*They giggle.*)

Shall I? Shall I?

ANGELA: Well, her's been asking for it.

AUDREY: (*Slyly*) *Am* I your Best Friend, Angela?

ANGELA: Yes, Aud. You be. You be!

(*Squeak–squeak–squeak.*)

9. THE WOODS

PETER, JOHN, WILLIE *and* RAYMOND *charging headlong through the trees, making the familiar Indian-brave whoop–whoop–whoo–oo–ooo–ooo.*

We race along with them, catching at the sheer physical excitement and abandon of a child's play. Until we reach the common at the edge of the woods.

10. THE OPEN GROUND

PETER *pulls up, hand at his side.*

PETER: Oof!

WILLIE: (*Pant*) Wassamatter? You had a start on us!

PETER: (*Gasp*) I got the stitch.

JOHN: Oy. And I have!

(*Panting and gasping they flop out on the tufty grass.* RAYMOND, *puffing, arrives at last, cowboy hat bobbing.*)

PETER: (*Jeer*) Slow coach!

RAYMOND: I was— (*Pant*) —g–g–guarding the back of us.

(*They loll about for a few seconds, each sucking on a blade of grass.*)

PETER: (*Eventually*) Anybody got em a match? Eh?

WILLIE: I ant.

JOHN: No. Nor me, wuss luck.

PETER: Ray?

RAYMOND: N–N–N—

(*And decides to shake his head.*)

PETER: (*Automatically*) K–Kuk–Katie.

JOHN: Donald Duck do sometimes get hold of a box. We ought to go and look for'n. Him'll give us a match if we let him play with us.

PETER: We could have us a good old fire. Set summat alight.

(*They brood about the possibility.*)

WILLIE: We could make a spark out of summat.

PETER: (*Dismissive*) Oy. I'll bet.

WILLIE: Oh, you can, mind! Like rubbing two stones together.

JOHN: It ant never worked for I.

PETER: No, nor nobody. Thow bist talking a lot of squit, Willie. As per u–sual.

WILLIE: No, that's right, mind. You can. Rub two stones together. What do you think they did before they had matches, cocky dick?

PETER: You mind I don't rub thy two ears together!

(*Sniggers all round, except from* WILLIE. *In the distance,* AUDREY *and* ANGELA *are approaching, pushing the squeaking pram.*)

JOHN: I thought it was two sticks you had to rub. Yeh. It's two sticks.

(*No response.*)

PETER: There ent nothing to touch a match.

(*Pause.*)

JOHN: (*Looking up*) Hark at thik bloody pram. Squeak. Squeak.

PETER: We don't want *them*, do us?

WILLIE: (*Shyly*) Angela's all right.

JOHN and PETER: (*Jeering crescendo*) Ooooooh! Ooooooh!

RAYMOND: (*Grin, grin*) Her's p–pup–pretty, is her Willie?

WILLIE: (*Squirming*) I mean her's all right for a girl.

PETER: Have you ever kissed her?

   (WILLIE *turns away, squirming.*)

WILLIE: Gettaway.

   (PETER *looks at the others.*)

PETER: I have, mind.

   (*They titter.*)

JOHN: (*Interested*) What's thou want to do that for?

PETER: Tasted like stro'berry jam.

   (*They roll about.*)

JOHN: Bet thou hasn't kissed Audrey though!

   (*More extravagant laughs.*)

WILLIE: Nobody never have, I'll bet.

PETER: No. And nobody ever will!

   (*Hoots of laughter.*)

RAYMOND: Hush up, mind. They be c–cu–coming. Her'll *hear* you.

JOHN: Frightened of her, are you Raymond?

   (*More sniggers.*)

WILLIE: Mind, her can't half pull your hair.

AUDREY: (*Calling*) Hell–o, Peter. How be, sweetheart.

THE OTHERS: Ooooooo!

PETER: What?

   (*He twists away, eyes swivelling with embarrassment.*)

AUDREY: (*Arriving*) I bin telling Angela about you and me.

PETER: I'll pull your bloody hair for you. I'll pull it all out!

AUDREY: (*To* ANGELA, *with a smirk*) See?

ANGELA: (*Severely*) Wipe thee nose, Peter.

PETER: Shut your chops.

   (*The boys get up, uncertain.*)

JOHN: Where be you two off, then?

AUDREY: Our cabin.

PETER: (*Jeer*) What cabin?

ANGELA: We got a cabin in the trees.

JOHN: Honest?

ANGELA: Him ent finished yet, though.

WILLIE: What do *you* want a cabin for?

PETER: They ent for girls, cabins ent.

AUDREY: To play House in.

JOHN: That's a sissy game, that is.

PETER: Mummies and bloody buggering Daddies.

(*They chortle.*)

ANGELA: I'll wash your mouth out with soap.

PETER: And I'll pull thik bit of ribbon out of your hair.

ANGELA: Smack him one, Aud.

PETER: We don't want you girls along of us.

AUDREY: Don't you want to see our cabin?

RAYMOND: We d–dud–don't want to p–pup–play house. Do us?

WILLIE: No we don't!

ANGELA: You could help us build it.

JOHN: How far have you got?

(AUDREY *and* ANGELA *look at each other.*)

AUDREY: We ant really started. Not yet.

ANGELA: (*Quickly*) 'S good idea, though. Ennit?

PETER: Not to play House in. We want summat better than that, Angela.

WILLIE: Like a Fort. With guns and that.

(RAYMOND *makes shooting noise with his lead pistol.*)

ANGELA: It can be a Fort when it's not a House.

WILLIE: For us soldiers, I mean. In case the Germans land.

RAYMOND: I be a M–Mur–Marine.

PETER: You can't be a Marine, Raymond.

RAYMOND: W–Why not? I c–cu–can if I d'want.

PETER: They won't let you be a Marine if you do stutter.

JOHN: That's the truth, Ray. Him's telling the truth.

RAYMOND: I can s–sus–stand on my head, though.

JOHN: That's right, mind. Him can.

PETER: Oy. I'll bet.

RAYMOND: How m–mu–much?

JOHN: Go on, Ray. Show him.

PETER: Till we do count up to ten.

RAYMOND: That's easy.

PETER: Ten *thousand*, I d'mean.

JOHN: Oh, that ent fair.

ANGELA: You've got to be fair.

PETER: A hundred, then.

WILLIE: What'll you give him if he does? You said as him couldn't.

AUDREY: Give him a penny.

WILLIE: Will you? Peter?

(PETER *is kicking up the ground, hands thrust deep in pockets.*)

PETER: (*Growl*) I can't go chucking my money about like that!

ANGELA: That's cos you ant got it. 'S all talk!

PETER: Ah, but what'll him give I if him don't last out? Eh? What about that, then?

RAYMOND: You can b–bub–borrow my knife.

PETER: Yeh? For how long?

RAYMOND: What'll you give *I*?

PETER: If you can do it, Raymond—

JOHN: Up to a hundred.

PETER: Keep out of it, you.

(*Again, there are signs of potential hostility between* JOHN *and* PETER.)

JOHN: Up to a hundred. That's what you said.

PETER: All right. All right. Up to a hundred.

RAYMOND: What'll you give?

PETER: If you can do't, Raymond, I'll give tha my ball of string. How about it?

RAYMOND: For k–ku–keeps?

PETER: For a day. I get your knife till tomorrow going-in time, if you *can't* do it, and you get my ball of string if you can. Right? Is that a deal?

RAYMOND: F–fuf–fair enough.

JOHN: Shake hands on it, then.

PETER: What?

JOHN: You gotta shake hands on a bet. That's a *rule*, that is.

(*And therefore holy writ.*)

PETER: Oh. Aye.

(*They solemnly shake hands.*)

63

JOHN: Starting when I go Ready–Steady–Go.
PETER: Come on, get on with it!
JOHN: Right, Raymond?
>   (RAYMOND *takes a deep breath and nods.*)
>   Rea–dy! (*Pause.*) Stea–dy! (*Pause.*) Go!
>   (RAYMOND *stands on his head.*)
WILLIE: One–two–three–four–five–six—
PETER: Not so fast! Not so fast!
WILLIE and JOHN: —seven–eight–nine–ten—
WILLIE, JOHN and ANGELA: (*Faster*)—eleven–twelve–thirteen—
PETER: (*Doggedly*) Se–ven–eigh–eight–ni–i–ne—
WILLIE, JOHN and ANGELA: (*Excited*)—fourteen–fifteen–sixteen–
>   seventeen–eighteen–nineteen–twenty—
PETER: (*Shouting*)—te–en el–ev–en twe–e–elve—
>   (AUDREY *decides where her loyalties lie.*)
PETER and AUDREY: —thir–ir–teen four–teeeen fif–teen—
WILLIE, JOHN and ANGELA: (*Frenzied*)—twenty-one–twenty-two–
>   twenty-three–twenty-four–twenty-five—
>   (*As their count gets faster, and* AUDREY*'s and* PETER*'s comically
>   slower,* PETER *breaks off and whispers urgently in* AUDREY*'s ear.
>   Her peeved, bespectacled, aggressive face breaks into a beautiful
>   smile.*)
>   —twenty-six–twenty-seven–twenty-eight–twenty-nine–
>   thirty–thirty-one–thirty-two–thirty-three—
>   (AUDREY *suddenly lets out a shattering and terrible scream. The
>   counting stops. Then—*)
AUDREY: (*Scream*) Blood! Blood!!
ANGELA: Wha—!
AUDREY: Coming out of Raymond's ear! Aaaaaaaaa!!
>   (RAYMOND, *startled and frightened, topples to the ground.*)
RAYMOND: Wha? What? Where?
>   (*He claps his hands to his ears.* PETER *jigs.*)
PETER: Your knife! Your knife! You gotta give me your knife!
JOHN: (*Angry*) Here. Let's see—
>   (*He examines* RAYMOND*'s ear.*)
AUDREY: (*Worried*) I thought it was. Honest. It looked like it.
>   Honest. Honest!

JOHN: (*Furious*) There yunt nothing there!

RAYMOND: (*Gulp*) You sure? J–John?

JOHN: Nothing! Bloody nothing! Not a drop!

PETER: Come on. Come on. Hand it over.

ANGELA: That's not fair, Peter.

PETER: (*Chortle*) Him didn't do it, did he? We shook hands on it. The knife's mine all right.

JOHN: You bloody cheat.

PETER: What?

JOHN: You bloody buggering cheat. I saw you whispering.

PETER: Now look—!

AUDREY: (*Scared*) I thought it was. Honest. Cross me heart. Honest.

JOHN: Well, it don't count. We'll start again. It don't count at all, Peter. So forget it, see.

PETER: Yes it do!

JOHN: Don't!

PETER: Do!

JOHN: Don't!

PETER: Shut your chops!

JOHN: Shut thine!

PETER: Mind I don't shut them for you, big mouth.

JOHN: And thee mind I don't shut yours, big head.

PETER: Yeh?

(JOHN, *unsure, licks his lips.*)

JOHN: Yeh.

(PETER, *still rather unsure himself, pokes him in the shoulder.*)

PETER: Oh, yeh?

AUDREY: (*Excited*) Give him one, Peter! Knock him down!

ANGELA: Don't let him, John. Hit him back!

JOHN: (*Not too confidently*) Cheat.

PETER: Say that once more and I'll knock your tith down your throat. (*Raises fist.*) Say it once more, that's all.

(JOHN *licks his lips. The others stand stock still, eyes blazing. Just as the excitement dies on their faces—*)

JOHN: Cheat.

11. THE FIGHT

PETER *frowns then lashes out.* JOHN *hits back, at once.*

A fight. The nearest equivalent being the long stand-up knock-down fist fights in the old western films. JOHN *and* PETER *thump and clout each other with increasing vigour. First one, then the other is ascendant. They move over yards of bumpy, grassy ground, grunting, gasping and slogging. The others give raucous support:* WILLIE, RAYMOND *and* ANGELA *for* JOHN, *and* AUDREY, *very loudly, for* PETER.

JOHN *is gradually winning.* PETER *is finally knocked backwards into a gorse bush.*

PETER: Ow! Ow! Ow!

JOHN: (*Pant*) Had enough, hast?

AUDREY: (*Scream*) Don't give in, Peter! Don't give in!

(*Despairingly,* PETER *pulls himself up and, head down, charges at* JOHN. JOHN, *triumphant, knocks him down. The others roar and shout and jig.* PETER *scrambles away, howling and sobbing, and starts to run and run.* AUDREY *goes after him, down the path towards the field and barn.*)

JOHN: (*Shout*) Run, babby, run!

AUDREY: (*Call*) Peter—!

PETER: (*Gasp, sob*) Bugger off. Leave I alone!

(*She stops, watching him recede. Her expression changes, horribly. She jumps up and down.*)

AUDREY: (*Scream*) Cowardy–cowardy–custard! Cowardy–cowardy–custard!

(PETER, *running, does not look back.* JOHN, *meanwhile, sits smirking, on the grass, a hero surrounded by back-patting congratulations.*)

JOHN: (*Cackle*) Didn't him go! Didn't him run! Eh?

WILLIE: You be Number Two now, John. That's for sure.

JOHN: Number Two! Oy—I be!

RAYMOND: You might even b–bub–beat W–Wallace.

ANGELA: Ne–ver.

JOHN: (*Gasp*) One day, perhaps. Thee's never know, mind. One of these days!

ANGELA: You got some blood or summat on your nose, John.

JOHN: (*Pleased*) Have I?

(ANGELA *gets a bit of rag from the pram.*)

ANGELA: Here. Let me wipe it off.

JOHN: No. Leave it on. (*Proudly*) Leave it as it is.

WILLIE: What'll your Mam say, though?

JOHN: Her'll give I one. (*Considers.*) Ay—wipe it off, Angie. Better had.

ANGELA: I be going to be a nurse.

JOHN: I shall be a soldier first. And then a boxer. There's a lot of Germans as is going to feel my fist afore very long.

WILLIE: And Japs.

JOHN: Oy. And bloody Japs.

(*Winces at* ANGELA's 'treatment'.)

Ow! Don't be so bloody rough!

(ANGELA *spits on the rag, and wipes again.*)

ANGELA: There. That's better. Ennit?

(WILLIE *is making aeroplane noises again, arms extended.*)

WILLIE: Vroooo–ooo–vooom!

(RAYMOND *uses his pistol.*)

RAYMOND: Rat-at–at–at–at-at! Got ya!

WILLIE: No you ant! You can't beat the RAF. Look at me, waggling my wings. Vroooooooom!

JOHN: No—and Peter can't beat me neither! (*He looks around.*) Where *is* Wallace Wilson today, any road?

WILLIE: Him ant bin seen, not nowhere.

(JOHN's *eyes have narrowed in speculation. Could he beat the fabulous Wallace? He decides, visibly, that it is just a dream.*)

JOHN: (*Laugh*) Well, wherever him is, he's up to summat or other, you can be sure o' that!

12. OUTSIDE THE BARN

PETER, *his face grubbily streaked with former tears, and his eye already beginning to swell, has reached the old barn.*

PETER: (*Hiss*) Just—you—wait. Just—you—wait. Just—you— wait.

(*He picks up a stone and angrily throws it away. Then enters the barn, moodily slouching.*)

13. THE BARN

DONALD *sees* PETER *come in. We see that* DONALD, *watchful, is hiding behind one of the thick wooden supports.*

    PETER *mooches about, whistling, tunelessly. Then—*

PETER: I'll bloody get him. I'll get him.

    (DONALD *coughs nervously.* PETER *whirls round.*)

DONALD: (*Scared*) H–Hello, Peter.

PETER: What you doing? Eh?

DONALD: N–Nothing, Peter. Honest.

    (PETER *scowls at him, then relaxes.*)

PETER: I been fighting.

DONALD: Who with?

PETER: (*Aggressively*) Who with? Who with? Mind thee own!

DONALD: (*Gulp*) Sorry.

PETER: John Harris. That's who with.

DONALD: Beat him, did you? (*Swallow.*) I expect.

PETER: (*Reluctant*) More like a draw.

DONALD: (*Craven*) Oh, I expect you beat him really.

PETER: (*Snarl*) Wos thou know about it!

DONALD: Nothing.

PETER: Quack! Quack! Quack! Goo on, flap your wings!

    (DONALD *looks at him, then beats his arms up and down, eyes moist.*)

DONALD: Quack! Quack! Quack! Quack!

PETER: Him had a couple of lucky punches. Sly bugger.

DONALD: Must have done. Him can't beat *you*.

    (PETER *feels his eye, glares at him.*)

PETER: I asked what you was doing in here, didn't I?

DONALD: Nothing much.

    (PETER *looks round, suspicious.*)

PETER: There ent no jam jars in here, is there?

DONALD: No. There yunt.

PETER: Willie said as you had a whole sackbag full yesterday.

DONALD: (*Nervously*) Then him's a liar.

PETER: (*Advancing*) Him said as you got ninepence out of 'em.

DONALD: No. Honest.

    (PETER *puts his fist to his mouth in a threatening gesture.*)

PETER: I'll knock your head in for tha, Donald Duck!

(DONALD *backs away, eyes wide with fear.*)

DONALD: I—I think I might know where there's some jam jars.

PETER: Tell us, then.

DONALD: You won't tell nobody else?

PETER: If you're having me on, mind—

DONALD: (*Quickly*) No—it's the truth. Honest it is, Peter. Honest.

PETER: Where be 'um, then?

DONALD: Well—you know behind the shop. In the garden.

PETER: Over the wall. Yeh.

DONALD: There's a bit of a shed there. By them old apple trees.

PETER: What about it?

DONALD: Well—(*Swallow*)—there's jam jars in there—I been mooching about.

PETER: You always be. Off on your own, like a loony.

DONALD: (*Nervous laugh*) I finds out things, though.

PETER: There's jam jars in there, is there?

DONALD: They must have come from the shop, see. And that's where they stores the empties.

PETER: What do you mean?

DONALD: Well, that's where Mr Hopkins puts the jam jars as is collected. (*Giggles.*)

(PETER *gapes at him, light dawning.*)

PETER: You mean—

(DONALD *hugs himself, his laughter rather manic.*)

DONALD: Yes! Mr Hopkins keeps the jars there till the lorry comes to take 'em away.

PETER: So they're all washed out and all.

DONALD: (*Giggle*) Yes!

PETER: There ent no horrible sticky on 'em nor nothing?

DONALD: Them be as good as new, Peter. Hundreds and hundreds of 'em.

(PETER *lets out a long whistle.*)

PETER: Bloom–in' heck!

DONALD: See! I bent no sissy, be I?

(PETER *still cannot quite take it in.*)

PETER: You mean, you took a sack of jars the shop had already

69

bought as empties and—by Gar! You got him to buy
'em off you all—over—again. . . !

DONALD: That's why you ant got to tell nobody. (*Looks anxiously
at* PETER.) You won't, Peter. You won't, will you?

PETER: You know what'll happen, doosn't?

DONALD: (*Anxiously*) What?

PETER: You'll go to gaol, won't you? Oy. That's what'll happen.

DONALD: You won't tell on me. Will you? Please! Oh, please!

PETER: (*Coldly*) What'll you give I?

(*Pause.*)

DONALD: (*Whisper*) Anything.

PETER: Can you get hold of any fags?

DONALD: N–no.

PETER: Don't your Dad smoke, then? Oh. I forgot.

DONALD: Yes.

PETER: Your Dad's *missing*, ent he? That's what they call it.

DONALD: The Japs have got him.

PETER: Him's as good as dead, then. Them Japs is the most
cruellest devils as ever walked.

DONALD: They won't beat our Dad. Our Dad ood never give in!

PETER: 'Xpect they'll tie him down on a great big hill of black
ants. That's what the Japs do. It was in the *Champion*. They
tried to do it to Rockfist Rogan and. . . . What you crying
for? Eh? What's the matter with you? Rockfist Rogan got
away, didn't he!

DONALD: (*Sob*) You oodn't like it if it was *your* Dad, oodya?

PETER: Don't be such a babby.

DONALD: My poor old Dad.

(PETER *looks at him, and the pain gets through.*)

PETER: No. I won't tell. Honest. I won't.

DONALD: I don't care. I don't care.

PETER: (*Frown*) Just wait till we get hold of them Japs, that's all.
Wicked buggers. Hey—listen—we got us a squirrel today!

DONALD: (*Brightening*) Did you? What—alive?

PETER: No. We had to knock him down out of a tree.

DONALD: They don't half bite, mind.

PETER: Once they get a hold of you they never ever let go.

You've had it then, all right. Got any matches?

DONALD: Matches?

(*He looks shifty again.*)

PETER: We could have a bit of a blaze, see.

DONALD: (*Hesitates.*) No. But—

(*But* PETER *is distracted.*)

PETER: My eye don't half hurt. Is it puffed up?

DONALD: 'Tis a bit.

PETER: The squirrel jumped right at me. Right at my face. What do you think of that?

DONALD: Honest?

PETER: Oh, I'm lucky to be still alive. The way him come at me.

DONALD: Did you cry?

PETER: I don't bloody cry. Now do I? I be going to be a parachuter.

DONALD: Do you like setting things on fire?

PETER: What?

DONALD: Only I might get hold of some matches.

PETER: You set your coal shed on fire, didn't you?

DONALD: Only a bit on't.

PETER: Bet that was good!

(DONALD *doubles up in a paroxysm of strangely frightened giggling.*)

DONALD: Oy! It was! It was that!

PETER: (*Suddenly*) Are you *hiding* in here?

DONALD: (*Stops laughing.*) No.

PETER: Come on. What have you done?

DONALD: I—nothing. But I ent going home for a bit.

PETER: That's daft, that is.

DONALD: No it ent.

(PETER *looks at him, intrigued.*)

PETER: What have you done? Eh?

DONALD: (*Furtive*) I ant done nothing.

(*The two boys examine each other.*)

PETER: Our Mam says her wish as her could have you. To stay, and that.

DONALD: (*Excited*) Do her? Do her?

71

PETER: But our Dad says as she is not to interfere.

DONALD: I ant done nothing *much*. Honest.

PETER: Tell us. Go on.

DONALD: I—well.

> (*Sudden sound of klaxon or siren from nearby—whoop–whoop–whoop–whooooop!*)

PETER: (*Excited*) That's from the Prisoner of War Camp! One of them bloody Ities have got loose.

DONALD: Or a German!

> (*They rush to the door. Klaxon still sounding.*)

14. AT DOOR OF BARN

PETER: There ent no Germans in thik camp, Donald. It's all Wops.

DONALD: I hope they don't catch him.

PETER: I hopes they do!

> (*Klaxon still sounding.*)

15. THE WOOD

JOHN, WILLIE, RAYMOND, ANGELA *and pram, and* AUDREY *have moved back into the trees. The klaxon or siren is sounding—and it seems very near.*

JOHN: Keep our eyes skinned. That's what we'll have to do.

ANGELA: Our Mam says we must come home when we d'hear that noise.

WILLIE: Oy—and Teacher said.

AUDREY: It's all right if we stick together.

> (*But they are beginning to frighten themselves.*)

RAYMOND: (*Peering about*) I got me kn–knife. That's summat.

WILLIE: Ities is good with knives, mind. They'll slit your throat as soon as look at ya!

> (ANGELA *lets out a wail.*)

ANGELA: I want to go home! I want to go ho–o–me!

JOHN: Don't cry, Angie. There's nothing to cry about. Honest.

AUDREY: And me. And I do!

WILLIE: P'raps we ought to get off these here path. Stop this pram from squeaking.

JOHN: Oy. Get into the trees a bit more. Find some cover.

AUDREY: Him won't *hurt* us, will he?

JOHN: (*Worried*) Don't expect him'll come along by here, any road. They've catched him by now, I'll bet.

WILLIE: Stuck a bayonet in him.

ANGELA: (*Shrill*) I hope! I hope!

JOHN: Shh, Angela! Not so much noise!

WILLIE: The Itie might hear us!

RAYMOND: (*Urgently*) L–Lul–Listen!!

(*They stand stock still in terror, listening to the sounds of the wood. A bird flies up in a sudden flutter of warning. RAYMOND loses his nerve and starts to run. The others stare wildly about and then bolt after him, leaving the pram behind. Gasping and panting with self-induced fear the five hurtle through the ferns and trees, keeping more or less together, leaving the pram unattended on the woodland paths.*)

16. THE HOLLOW

The five plunge for safety into a natural, grassy, scooped-out hollow in the midst of the trees. They huddle together, breathless and scared.

JOHN: Him won't find us down in here.

ANGELA: You sure?

JOHN: Ne–ver. 'Course him won't.

WILLIE: We didn't stand a chance out there on the path.

JOHN: (*Unsure*) This is nice and safe. Ennit?

AUDREY: What did you hear, Raymond?

RAYMOND: Him!

JOHN: Did—did you *see* him?

RAYMOND: I d–du–don't know.

ANGELA: I wanna go home.

JOHN: We'll have to stay here a bit.

WILLIE: F'r how long, though?

RAYMOND: (*Whisper*) Till d–dark—shall us?

JOHN: They'll have the guards out after him. They'll soon catch him.

AUDREY: What'll they do to him?

JOHN: Shoot him.

AUDREY: Good job.

WILLIE: Where's the pram?

73

ANGELA: Oh. Oh. The pram! And Dinah! (*Cry*) Pore little Dinah . . .

JOHN: It won't hurt where it is.

ANGELA: (*Wail*) But her'll be fright–ened!

WILLIE: Hold your hosses!

(*But she is sobbing.*)

JOHN: Oh we'll go and get the pram. In a minute.

WILLIE: Who will?

(JOHN *licks his lips.*)

JOHN: All of us. It'll be all right if'n we stick together. Eh?

AUDREY: (*Belligerent*) Never mind the pram!

WILLIE: How long we going to stay here, that's what I wanna know.

RAYMOND: (*Whisper*) Must be d–du–dinner time.

WILLIE: Have a look over the top, John.

JOHN: (*Alarmed*) What?

WILLIE: See if there's anybody moving about up there.

JOHN: In a minute.

(*He sees* AUDREY *looking at him, and lowers his eyes.*)

AUDREY: You're not frightened. Are you?

JOHN: 'Course not!

AUDREY: Wallace Wilson 'ood go up and have a look.

JOHN: In a minute, I said. Shut your mouth, Audrey.

AUDREY: Oy—and *Peter* would an' all.

JOHN: (*Mutter*) Shut your cakehole.

RAYMOND: L–Lul–Listen!!

(RAYMOND'*s way of saying this is, again, of such chilling urgency that the others freeze in sheer terror. A trembling pause. Woodland sounds. Wood pigeons coo–coo.*)

WILLIE: (*Whisper*) Raymond? What is it?

(*Eyes wide,* RAYMOND *clutches at the nearest arm.*)

RAYMOND: (*Desperate*) Hark—!

(*Sure enough—the sound of someone running—crashing heavily through the woodland undergrowth. The five huddle closer in desperation, whimpering. A figure breaks to the top of the hollow, socks down to the ankles, bootlace undone. It is* PETER.)

PETER: What you doing down in there?

JOHN: Peter! (*Shamefaced*) We thought—
AUDREY: We thought you was that Wop.
PETER: (*Snigger*) Me? That's a good 'un!
WILLIE: Didn't you hear that siren thing?
   (PETER *is clambering down.*)
PETER: Hear it? 'Course I heard it. I byun't deaf, be I? I was
   looking for tha'.
JOHN: What for?
   (PETER *looks at him.*)
PETER: (*Pleased*) Frightened—was you?
JOHN: Me? 'Course I warn't.
AUDREY: (*Hotly*) Yes you was! Yes him was! We been bloody
   crying and all down in here.
JOHN: *You* have, you mean.
PETER: Donald Duck is trembling like a jelly.
WILLIE: Where is he?
PETER: The barn. Him oodn't leave. Come th'on, I said. Let's go
   and catch the Itie. No, him oodn't. Went back and hid in
   the corner.
JOHN: The sissy.
ANGELA: And you be, John.
AUDREY: You done the same!
JOHN: (*Stung*) That's 'cos we had you girls along, ennit? Ennit
   Willie? Ennit Raymond? We boys wasn't frightened, was
   us?
WILLIE: No!
RAYMOND: 'C–Cu–Course not.
AUDREY: (*Jabbing finger*) You wouldn't even have a peep, John.
ANGELA: *And* you made me leave my pram!
PETER: (*Pleased*) 'S that right?
JOHN: (*Annoyed*) I got to look a'ter 'em, enn I? This 'ere I–talian
   or Wop or whatever he calls hisself, might have a knife.
   Have you thought of that?
PETER: Ne–ver!
   (*But a flicker of anxiety crosses his face.*)
RAYMOND: No, that's right m–mum–mind.
JOHN: And what if him's out for blood?

WILLIE: *English* blood.

(PETER *gapes at them.*)

PETER: I hadn't thought of that. Him could have *got* I!

WILLIE: Stuck a knife in you.

PETER: (*Looking about*) Him won't never find us in these here woods. Will he?

JOHN: He killed two or dree guards to get out of the camp. Slit their throats.

AUDREY: (*Half excited*) Did he?

(ANGELA *wails.*)

WILLIE: (*Frown*) How do you know, John?

JOHN: That's what I heard, any road.

PETER: By Gar!

WILLIE: But you been with us all the time! You ant bin out of our sight, John.

AUDREY: You been with us all the time!

JOHN: No I ant.

AUDREY: Yes you bloody have!

JOHN: Even if I have, it's obvious, ennit?

PETER: Is it?

JOHN: They don't just open the gate and let a prisoner of war out—now do 'um?

WILLIE: No. 'Course not.

JOHN: Him'd have to kill—oodn't he?

PETER: That's right. That's it. You have got it!

RAYMOND: (*Worried*) L–Lul–Let's go home.

JOHN: Nobody's stopping you.

(RAYMOND *looks at the others.*)

RAYMOND: Ent you c–cu–coming—?

WILLIE: Shall us?

ANGELA: Yes!

JOHN: Nobody's stopping you.

(PETER *looks at* JOHN, *and decides to line up with him.*)

PETER: Nobody's stopping you!

ANGELA: (*Tearful*) What about my poor little Dinah? Her'll cry and cry and cry.

WILLIE: Well, I'm not going out there on me own.

RAYMOND: N–Nun–Nor me.

AUDREY: Yes, but what about her bloody doll?

ANGELA: Stop cussing.

JOHN: Shall we go and get'm, Peter?

PETER: What? Me and you?

JOHN: We be the best two.

ANGELA: You can't leave us! You can't go on your own!

AUDREY: Somebody's got to go.

WILLIE: (*Nervous*) You won't be long, though? You *will* come back?

RAYMOND: P–Pup–Please hurry up.

JOHN: Just keep your heads down.

PETER: And don't move.

JOHN: Don't make a sound.

PETER: Good job you got us, I reckon Number Two and Number Three.

(JOHN *looks at him.*)

JOHN: Which is Number Two?

(*Slight, sad pause.*)

PETER: You be.

JOHN: Peter's right. It's a good job you got us. (*Warmly*) Come on Peter, old pal—

PETER: (*Anxious*) You sure?

JOHN: We gotta take a chance.

PETER: Oy. Come on then.

JOHN: Wait here, you lot. (*To* PETER) Come on.

(*But they haven't moved.*)

PETER: Together, shall us?

JOHN: Oy. Together.

(*They look at each other, swallow, and, as on a beat, scramble up out of the hollow. Leaving four scared companions.*)

17. TREES BEYOND THE HOLLOW

Moving cautiously, and whispering, JOHN *and* PETER *move through the trees.*

JOHN: (*Whisper*) If you hear anything—

PETER: Yes? What?

JOHN: We'll throw ourselves flat on the ground.

PETER: What for?

JOHN: That's what soldiers do.

PETER: Yeh. Right.

> (*Silently, they move forward in a comic parody of pantomimic creeping.*)

18. THE HOLLOW

The four left behind are tense and nervous.

WILLIE: (*Low voice*) I don't reckon they be safe out there. Him'll jump out on 'um.

ANGELA: (*Close to tears again*) Will they come back?

AUDREY: (*Snarl*) 'Course they will.

> (*Silence. Birdsong.*)

WILLIE: I don't trust 'em. I don't trust 'em at all. They'll run home for their dinner.

AUDREY: Shhh!

> (*They hold silence. Tense. Blackbird's warning trill. Suddenly, a blood-curdling cry, off, through the trees.*)

JOHN: (*Off*) No–o–o–oo–oo! Aaaaaagh! Him have got me! Aaaaagh! The knife!

PETER: (*Off*) Keep away! Keep away! No–o–o–oo! Aaaaaaaaaagh! I be done for!

> (*Wide-eyed and trembling with shock and terror,* WILLIE, RAYMOND, ANGELA *and* AUDREY *cling to each other, moaning and sobbing.*)

19. TREES BEYOND THE HOLLOW

Out in the wood, PETER *and* JOHN *(who have decided that nobody is about) are rolling on the ground, helpless with suppressed, belly-aching laughter. A moment before either of them is able to speak.*

PETER: (*Eventually*) Ho–hoo–hoo—do you—hee–hee.

JOHN: Do I—ho–ho—do I—hee–hee–hee—do I what? Ho–ho–ho . . .

> (*They have to break off for more near hysterical laughter.*)

PETER: (*At last*) Do you think— (*Gasp*) —do you think they heard?

JOHN: They—they heard all right.
(*And both explode with helpless but suppressed laughter again.*)

20. THE HOLLOW
The four are in painful desperation. ANGELA *is weeping.* RAYMOND *has his hands to his ears, eyes screwed shut, moaning.* AUDREY *is curled up in foetal position and then* WILLIE—
WILLIE: Help! Help! He–e–elp! Dad! Dad! Help!
(*The others decide to do the same.*)
ALL: Help! Help! Help!

21. THE OLD BARN
'DONALD DUCK' *sits on trough or cartwheel, striking matches one after another from a box of 'England's Glory'. He lets each match burn down until it almost reaches his fingers, then drops it quickly. All the time he glances round, anxiously.*

He strikes another match, watches the flame. A new expression flares in his eyes. He looks round at the heap of straw—so intently that the match burns his fingers.
DONALD: Oh!
(*And drops the match quickly.*)

22. THE HOLLOW
The cries at peak desperation.
WILLIE, RAYMOND, AUDREY and ANGELA: Help—help—help!
(*And the pram comes crashing down on top of them. Shrieking and shouting in panic, the four scramble up out of the hollow as fast as they can. To be met by* PETER and JOHN, *pointing and whooping with delight and derision.*)
JOHN: Hee! Hee! Gotcha! Gotcha!
PETER: Hoo! Hoo! Had ya—didn't us! Didn't us!
(AUDREY *goes wild. She leaps at* PETER, *nails clawing, hands flailing.*)
AUDREY: You devil! You devil!
(*The violence of her momentum knocks* PETER *to the ground.*)
PETER: Get off! Get—off!
(*But she pummels him hard. The others watch, open-mouthed.*)

AUDREY: I'll bash you up! Bash you up! Bash you up!

PETER: Ow! Ow! Ow! Audrey—no! No!

JOHN: Girls ent s'posed to do that.

AUDREY: Bash–you–up!

PETER: Get off—off!

(*With a desperate heave, he rolls over on top of her and pinions her wrists.*)

JOHN: Good old Peter!

PETER: Give in? Going to stop?

AUDREY: (*Shrill*) I shall tell our Mam!

ANGELA: Yes! And I ool!

JOHN: Oh, come on. 'Sonly a bit of fun.

WILLIE: Fun!

RAYMOND: Wasn't very n–nun–nice for us!

PETER: (*Gasp*) Give in? Audrey? Or I'll spit, mind!

(*He makes a bubble of spit.*)

AUDREY: No!

PETER: I'll spit on thee glasses, Aud. I will.

AUDREY: (*Gasp*) I be a *girl*, mind. A girl!

ANGELA: You dirty devil, Peter!

(WILLIE *suddenly shouts and points.*)

WILLIE: Look! Look!

(*They all stop, and look.*)

JOHN: What is it?

WILLIE: (*Gurgle*) The Itie! And him have got a gurt long knife!

(*Frozen horror.*)

PETER: (*Quake*) W–Where. . . ?

(WILLIE *gives a gleeful little jig.*)

WILLIE: Gotcha! Gotcha!

PETER: (*Furious*) I shall smack thou one!

AUDREY: See! See! 'Tent very nice, is it biggie boots!

JOHN: (*Just to be sure*) You didn't see nothing, did you?

WILLIE: No. But I might have. Him might be there for all we do know.

(*The thought is extremely sobering for all of them.*)

RAYMOND: P'raps him's l–lul–looking at us n–nun–now.

AUDREY: Oh my God.

JOHN: (*Frown*) We have made a hell of a racket, ant us?

PETER: Him might have heard.

WILLIE: (*Twitching*) *Would* have heard.

ANGELA: Oh let's get on home. Let's get away from here!

PETER: Oy. We'd better. Shall us, John?

WILLIE: Hadn't us, John?

JOHN: (*Whisper*) Don't talk so loud.

(*They all look at each other.*)

PETER: Come on! I byunt stopping. Let's run for it!

(*And without more ado he bolts. The six, in ragged formation, crash through ferns and undergrowth.*)

23. THE OLD BARN

'DONALD DUCK' *stooping down, a small pile of burnt-out matches beside him, strikes yet another, cups his hand to shield the flame, and tries to light the straw. It seems this is not the first attempt: some of the dampish straw is charred. And the flame flickers, flares, dies.*

DONALD: (*Intense*) Aw, come on. Come on.

(*He strikes another 'England's Glory'*)

If it don't take this time, the Japs have won. The bloody flaming buggering flaming bloody buggering Japs have won!

(*He holds it to the straw. A small flame flutters, almost dies, then very slowly curls and licks along the edge of the straw. Crackle–crackle–crackle. Excited now, jigging a bit, sucking on his fingers, DONALD watches it. Then, with cupped hands, he feeds the little fire with some of the drier hay.*)

(*Trance-like*) Come on, come on, come, come on, come.

(*And it is coming on.*)

24. OPEN GROUND, AND FIELD

JOHN, PETER, WILLIE, RAYMOND, ANGELA *and* AUDREY *out of breath, have run from the woods, across the common, into the field.*

The barn is up ahead.

JOHN *slows.*

JOHN: Oof! I be puffed!

PETER: (*Gasp*) I could keep going for another hundred miles.

WILLIE: (*Pant*) Oy, I'll bet!

ANGELA: (*Gasp*) We kept up, didn't us?

AUDREY: (*Pant*) My glasses is all steamed over.

RAYMOND: (*Gasp*) F–Fuf–Four eyes.

AUDREY: (*Sings*) When the mum–moon shines
    Over the cuc–cow shed—

JOHN: Oh, stop arguing for God's sake. We be safe now, ben us?
    Too fast for thik bloody Itie any road!

PETER: Wonder if Donald Duck is still hiding in the barn?

WILLIE: Poor old Quack Quack.

    (*They laugh.*)

RAYMOND: Let's p–pup–pretend t–to . . .

JOHN: Be the I–talian. Oy. That's a good 'un!

PETER: It have come off twice!

JOHN: Three times lucky!

PETER: (*Chortle*) Frighten him to death.

    (WILLIE *puts on a deep voice.*)

WILLIE: (*Mimics*) Who is-a da there! I gotta da knife-a!

    (*They laugh in delight.*)

PETER: (*Impressed*) That's good that is, Willie.

WILLIE: (*Pleased*) You know, like Musso the Wop in the comic.

JOHN: Creep up on him—eh? That's a good 'un.

PETER: Last one to the barn is a cissy!

    (*And away he scampers.*)

25. THE OLD BARN

DONALD, *eyes smarting, stands back in awe at the size of the fire he has created.*

    The flames are engulfing the greater mass of hay in about a quarter of the barn, and a few tongues of fire are stretching towards the roof.

    Eyes wide, mouth open, DONALD *begins to back towards the door, which is kept half open by a large stone.*

DONALD: (*With hate*) Burn you bugger! Burn! Burn!

    (*The flames seem to swell and belly out suddenly.* DONALD, *in alarm, scurries for the door. And it slams shut—bang!—*)

26. OUTSIDE THE BARN

Giggling with excitement, the other six have slammed shut the door,
putting the stone back against it, and further holding it shut with six pairs
of hands.

WILLIE: (*Shout*) Who—is—a—there! I gott-a da knife-a to slit-a
da throat-a!

(*From inside,* DONALD *is pushing against the door until it rattles.*)

DONALD: (*Scream, from inside*) Open the door! Help! Help!

PETER: (*Delighted*) Hark at him!

(*Rattle—thump—scream.*)

WILLIE: (*Shout*) I gott-a da knife-a.

DONALD: (*Scream, from inside*) Help! Help!

(*Smoke seeping under door.*)

JOHN: Him have got a fire going, the devil.

PETER: And him told me him didn't have no matches! Hark at
him, though. Good, ennit?

(*They are all laughing.*)

DONALD: (*Scream inside*) Open the door! Please! Please! Open the
door! Plea—ea—ease!

27. THE OLD BARN

In a dreadful panic, and unable to think, DONALD *retreats from the door*
to try to get out of the window. Trapping himself.

The flames drive in a leaping crackle towards the door.

As DONALD, *wildly dashing about, screams, a roof timber collapses*
beside him in a shower of sparks.

28. OUTSIDE THE BARN

Looks of consternation on six faces.

WILLIE *is the first to realize fully.*

WILLIE: Quick! Quick!

JOHN: What? Wha—?

WILLIE: (*Sob*) Open the door! Open it!

ANGELA: (*Scream*) Open it!

(*In a flustered frenzy they drag open the barn door. Flames leap out*
towards the air. They recoil in terror and horror, screaming and
shouting.)

83

WILLIE: (*Sob*) Donald! Donald! Oh Donald!

PETER: (*Crying*) Come on out! Donald! Come on, old pal!

JOHN: I shall tell his Mam! I shall! Silly great fool!

WILLIE: Oh don't do that! No!

JOHN: (*Yell*) I shall! I shall tell his Mam!

ALL: Donald! Donald—!

> (DONALD *is briefly glimpsed through the flames, gesticulating, then wholly engulfed. The barn is being gutted, and the tiles slide off the roof. In terror, the six run away as the inside of the barn implodes into flame. They run, run, back into the tall grass of the field.*)

29. THE FIELD

They sit, obscured by long grass, curiously apart, badly shaken.

RAYMOND: P–Poor old Donald!

ANGELA: He should've—he should've come out—!

AUDREY: 'Twasn't our fault!

JOHN: We'll be sure to get the blame though. You can bank on it.

PETER: I byunt going to get the blame for it. I never did anything. I wasn't even holding the door.

ANGELA: Yes you were!

PETER: No I wasn't! I was bloody miles away!

AUDREY: You was with *me*, Peter. Wasn't you with me?

> (*Pause.*)

WILLIE: We was all together.

ANGELA: Miles away!

> (*Pause.*)

WILLIE: What?

ANGELA: Well, we were! Hiding in the trees, weren't we?

JOHN: That's right. We didn't see nothing.

PETER: (*Eager*) We don't know nothing about it, do us?

> (*But they start to cry, overwhelmed.*)

RAYMOND: Poor old Quack Quack.

> (*We see them in long shot, sobbing. The barn burns.*)

VOICE: Into my heart, an air that kills
   From yon far country blows
   What are those blue remembered hills?

What spires, what farms are those?
That is the land of lost content,
I see it shining plain.
The happy highways where I went
And cannot come again.

Joe's Ark

Joe's Ark was first shown on BBC TV on 14 February 1974. The cast was as follows:

JOE	Freddie Jones
LUCY	Angharad Rees
JOHN	Christopher Guard
COMEDIAN	Denis Waterman
SALLY	Patricia Franklin
PREACHER	Edward Evans
DOCTOR	Clive Graham
CUSTOMER	Emrys Leyshon
WOMAN CUSTOMER	Margaret John
CHEF	Colin Rix
PAKISTANI	Azad Ali
Director	Alan Bridges
Producer	Graeme McDonald
Designer	Stuart Walker

My late father, to whom I grow closer and closer in that parish which allows the living to grasp the no longer cold hand of the beloved dead, used to have great difficulty in holding back a quite untoward levity when attending a funeral. This was not because of any lack of sympathy for those who were mourning, but rather from an elliptical or allusive recognition that there is something jauntily comical about our mortality which cannot be caught by starched faces or sadly beautiful ceremonies. I think we are all far less frightened of death than custom and language delude us into thinking we are, an error further compounded by our understandable assumption that it would be morbid to consider the matter with any great rigour (no pun absolutely intended) until we have to. Like Justice Shallow, we put such thoughts aside with a briskly sensible jollity: 'Certain, 'tis certain; very sure, very sure. Death, as the Psalmist saith, is certain to all, all shall die. How a good yoke of bullocks at Stamford fair?'

It is Eros and not Thanatos who mostly cavorts upon our screens, and I do not doubt that it is more entertaining to see someone pretending to make love than someone else pretending to die. (Excluding *violent* death, of course, which is used by film-makers as yet another substitute for uncovered buttocks, expiring gasps, and, yes, the bollocks if not the bullocks at Stamford fair.) For much the same reason, I chose a beautiful young girl, rather than an ugly old man with warts on his nose, to lay my small blooms at the feet of the dark angel. The old and the unlovely are wise to insist that we do not love them.

I have read, and I assume it to be true, that Lazarus was considered to be a figure of horror in the Middle Ages. The idea that one should be made to come back again after having already gained what used to be called the far shore was thought to be too intolerable for endurance, and I suppose we have only

89

to look at the spectral figure of Edward Heath as he sits with awful mien on his bench in the Commons to get some faint equivalent of such a piteous state. It is the finality of death, and not our lack of evidence about what happens in whatever new condition which follows, to which we mortals need to address ourselves.

And this *is* the question the central character manages to bring and keep to the fore, though the healthily alive around her find many ways of evading or denying it, whatever their prior beliefs appear to have been. But since the question is a serious and also rather comical one, the two intruders I especially did not want to come creeping up on me were Pathos and Sentimentality. I threw them out of the room several times, but, of course, they sneaked back in again, and I am unhappily aware of the sweet cloy of their breath upon the back of my neck as I reread the play.

Even so, the cheerful brutality which has largely displaced my former tender disgust is beginning to come to the fore in *Joe's Ark*. I noticed in rehearsal that almost everyone concerned seemed intent upon excavating the solemnity rather than the intrinsic comedy of the piece, but I was at that time either too ill or too diffident to do anything much about it and did not go again. Writers, and not directors, are the kings of electronic drama, but only if they insist upon occupying the throne. In any case, it is difficult at the best of times not to be lugubrious in a BBC rehearsal room. Lazarus, he never wrote a play.

Joe's Ark

I. A PET SHOP, WELSH TOWN

There are roll-up shutters at the big window, but they do not fit too well, so a thin gruel of light dribbles into the shop from the top and sides of the shutters.

Sound of rain.

Sitting weirdly still in the weird half-light on a high old-fashioned stool in the middle of the little shop is JOE, *the proprietor, late forties or older, small, blank, hunched-up into himself, surrounded by animals in cages, pens, boxes, perches, hutches, and tanks, always visible.*

VOICE OF PREACHER: And God looked upon the earth, and, behold, it was corrupt; for all flesh had corrupted his way upon the earth. And it repented the Lord that he had made man on the earth, and it grieved him at his heart.

(JOE *takes out a handkerchief and wipes his nose, then slowly looks round the animals of the shop, their eyes gleaming in the half-light.*)

And God said: The end of all flesh is come before me, for the earth is filled with violence through them. And behold, I, even I, do bring a flood of waters upon the earth to destroy all flesh wherein is the breath of life.

(*Golden hamsters in sawdust-floored cage. Guinea pig, scratching at plywood floor. Twitching Dutch rabbit.*)

And the Lord said: I will destroy man whom I have created from the face of the earth: both man and beast and the creeping thing and the fowls of the air, for it repenteth me that I have made them.

(*He gets down from stool and goes across to a cage.*)

And all the flesh died that moved upon the earth, both of fowl and of cattle and of beast and of every creeping thing that creepeth upon the earth. And of every man.

(JOE *goes back to listen at foot of stairs.*)

All in whose nostrils was the breath of life, of all that was in the dry land *died.*

Joe's Ark

(*Silence—except for the rain outside. The pride of the shop, a brilliant cockatoo, appears to shift uneasily on its perch in the corner.*)

JOE: (*Hiss*) Let it rain! Please God let it pour! Let it go on raining! For ever and ever and ever!

(*Fractional pause. Then, weird and sudden, the big cockatoo lets out a bloodcurdling shriek.*)

Shut up! Shut up! You'll wake Lucy, you feathery idiot!

(*The bird shrieks again.* JOE *looks back and crosses to foot of stairs. He listens, alert.*)

2. A SMALL BEDROOM DIRECTLY ABOVE THE SHOP

LUCY, *about 18, jerks in the bed as though in response to the bird's melodramatic screech. She looks around, blinking, almost gasping, startled out of a fretful or feverish sleep.*

She is Joe's daughter, and she is very ill.

She frowns, confused. Then reaches for a glass of juice on bedside table, hand trembly. But she can't make it. She sinks back on to the propped-up pillows, listening to the torrential rain.

LUCY: (*Mutter*) Sunday. . . ! Sod it. Sod it.

3. SHUTTERED SHOP DIRECTLY BELOW

Comically, yet disturbingly, JOE *addresses the cockatoo, which shifts from claw to claw.*

JOE: (*Strong Welsh accent*) You just wake her up, boyo, that's all! You wake her up with that big mouth of yours and I'll wring your scrawn-y neck for you. Do you hear? Eh?

(JOE *listens, cocking his head like the bird does. Then relaxes. But a few of the other animals, restless, begin to make noises.*)

Keep quiet, all of you. Stupid, thoughtless creatures, the lot of you. Don't like the rain, do you? (*Grim chuckle.*) No. You don't that. You don't like it. Perhaps it won't stop, eh? Perhaps this time it won't stop.

(*Knock–knock–knock at shop doorway.* JOE *starts, jerks, at the sound.*)

(*Flat*) Go away. Just go away.

(*But the knocking continues, more loudly. Hissing under his breath,*

92

JOE *is forced to go to the bolted door.*)
Stop it! Stop it! You'll wake her up. You'll wake her.
(*He pushes open the shop door.*)

4. SHOP DOORWAY

It is a young man hammering on the door, in the rain.

JOE: Stop this banging, will you! It's a Sunday. We're shut.
Shut! Go away!

JOHN: I—no I haven't come—I'm not a customer—

JOE: Says Closed, doesn't it? Can't you flaming read? All that
noise!

JOHN: Please—I've come to see Lucy.

JOE: (*Faint*) Lucy?

JOHN: I'm a friend of Lucy's and—

JOE: (*Abrupt*) Ill. She's ill.

JOHN: I know. But. She—

JOE: Can't see nobody. No.

JOHN: I thought— (*Gulp.*) When I saw the curtains shut and the
shutters down and—

JOE: (*Sharp*) You thought *what*?

JOHN: (*Evasive*) Look—I'm awfully wet and—I've come a long
way—

JOE: Closed curt–ains?

JOHN: I didn't mean to—to—

JOE: (*Harsh*) She's not going to die!

JOHN: N–No—I—of course not . . .

JOE: (*Very hostile*) Then what do you mean—closed curtains?

JOHN: I didn't mean— I've hitched down from Oxford.
(*They examine each other.* JOHN *is dripping wet, and oddly fearful.*)

JOE: (*Grudgingly*) All right. You'd better come in, I suppose.

JOHN: Th–Thank you. I—

5. THE PET SHOP

JOE: Wipe your feet, mun!

JOHN: Oh. Sorry. Yes.

JOE: Don't you have doormats at Oxford, then.

JOHN: (*Very awkward*) I beg your pardon. I— It *is* Mr Jones, isn't it? Lucy's father—?

JOE: I don't want wet and mud all over my shop, do I now?

JOHN: No.

(*They look at each other.*)

JOE: She's not going to die!

JOHN: No.

(*Silence.*)

JOE: Oxford—did you say?

JOHN: Yes . . . we kind of—Lucy and I . . .

(JOE *moves away, circling the counter.*)

JOE: (*Savage*) She should never have gone there! Never!

JOHN: I did try to telephone on my way. It was engaged all the—

JOE: Off the hook.

JOHN: Oh.

JOE: It's a Sunday. No business on a Sunday.

JOHN: (*Sudden rush*) I love her, Mr Jones. I want to see her please.

(*Pause.*)

JOE: (*More gentle*) Who are you? What's your name?

JOHN: John. John Brady. I—we got to know each other—to—um—care about each other at Ox—last term. She—

(JOE *cuts him off.*)

JOE: Never heard of you. She's never so much as mentioned your name.

JOHN: (*Hurt*) Oh. I—no. She—

JOE: I don't want her *bothered*, see.

JOHN: (*Cautious*) Is she—um—is there any change in—um—

JOE: (*Decisive*) Holding her own. She's holding her own. *Definitely.*

(*Then, as though* JOHN *were not there,* JOE *goes and sits back on his stool, abstracted. Still very wet,* JOHN *stands, awkward and unhappy, in the middle of the shop.*)

JOHN: Is there—can I do anything. . . ?

JOE: (*Snap*) Do?

JOHN: I mean, help in any way—you see, I—(*Gesturing towards cage.*)

94

JOE: Feed the little alligators.

JOHN: Pardon?

JOE: Over there. In that tank.

JOHN: Alligators?

JOE: There's some gentles in that big tin on the far shelf.

JOHN: (*Wretchedly confused*) Gentles?

JOE: Maggots! Bluebottle maggots. I thought you said you went
to Oxford!

JOHN: (*Distraught*) I don't know anything about *maggots*, Mr
Jones.

JOE: The world is full of maggots. You don't have to have a good
education to know that! Out there—it's *all* maggots. I wish I
never had to open the door.
(*Pause.*)

JOHN: Mr Jones?
(JOE *looks at him, his expression changing.*)

JOE: Get your coat off. You're soaked, boyo. Dripping.
(*Relieved by the change of tone* JOHN *pulls off his wet jacket.*)
Hang it up on that hook. There. The one with the dog leads
dangling.

JOHN: Yes. Thank you. It was raining all the way down . . .

JOE: Raining pouring!

JOHN: I couldn't get lifts very easily. People don't like to stop in
the wet.

JOE: Let it rain!

JOHN: Pardon?

JOE: Let it rain and rain and rain!
(*Pause.*)

JOHN: (*Unhappy*) It—it's not very light in here, is it?

JOE: Light enough!

JOHN: But how can y—
(*The cockatoo shrieks as* JOHN *starts to speak. He is in a bad dream.*
JOE *again scurries malevolently towards the bird.*)

JOE: Shut it, I said! Shut it up, else I'll twist your head off, you
squawking great fool!
(*The big, bright bird cocks its head, alert and beady-eyed.*)

JOHN: (*Miserable*) I'm sorry I've called at—at—such a bad time

Joe's Ark

for you—but—

(JOE *looks back at him, not without sympathy.*)

JOE: I thought you was somebody else, son. I'm not—very hospitable today. I'm sorry.

JOHN: That's OK. I understand . . .

JOE: No, I thought you was somebody who I don't want to set foot in this house. Not ever!

(JOE *again drifts off into silence.*)

JOHN: (*Nervous*) Can I put this lamp on, Mr Jones?

JOE: What for?

JOHN: It's getting awfully dark in here and—

JOE: Yes, yes. Put it on. What's the odds! You're not paying for it.

(JOHN *switches on the lamp by the big tank of goldfish.*)

JOHN: Lucy is—she's asleep now, is she? Because if it's at all possible I'd like to—

JOE: (*Abrupt*) Do you believe in the Bible?

JOHN: (*Startled*) I—well—you can't really say Yes or No, just like that . . .

JOE: Why not?

(*His suddenly intent look signals 'Caution' to* JOHN.)

JOHN: Because—there are many different kinds of experience or hope or despair gathered together over many thousands of years in—

JOE: (*Impatient*) I don't!

(*Slight pause.*)

JOHN: Don't you?

JOE: Yesterday I did. Last night I did. And this morning I did, when I went to Chapel. We've got a good preacher here. Dan Watkins. A treat to listen to on a wet Sunday. But—

(*He shakes his head slowly.*)

JOHN: Is it anything to do with— I mean—

JOE: Lucy?

(JOHN *gives a quick, nervous, bobbing series of nods.* JOE *leans nearer to him, and speaks confidentially.*)

I walked out! Right in the middle of Daniel's sermon. Lucy? She— (*Gets up.*) On about Noah, see. The one just man in

96

those bad times. (*He circles cages.*) So God let *him* live
and killed all the rest, men, women, kids, cattle, fowls, the
lot. Well, then!

JOHN: It's a—legend. A sort of fable . . .

JOE: (*Contemptuous*) Leg–end! It's in the Bible, ennit? What do
you mean, legend. Either it *is* or it is *not* so.
(*Stands, leaning on end of counter.*)

JOHN: What do the— What do the doctors say now, about Lucy?
Do they hold out much—
(*He doesn't finish.* JOE *goes around counter and up to shelves
behind.*)

JOE: The world's as bad now as it ever was before the flood.

JOHN: Will she go back into hospital or what?

JOHN: Yet while the wicked flourish all over the globe, *she* has to—
(*Again, it cannot be said.*)

JOHN: Please may I see her?

JOE: Well you can keep that sort of God. It came into my head
like a shout. Looked around at all those faces, lapping it up
like cats at a saucer and—up the stairs, there. Door on the
left at the top, directly overhead her room is.
(JOHN *darts across the shop, eager.*)
Knock on the door. Gentle, mind! Gentle. Else I'll—

JOHN: Yes, Mr Jones. Yes.
(*He goes up the stairs.*)

JOE: What you got that bag for?

JOHN: Oh, I've got—there's a present here for Lucy. A book.

JOE: (*Bitter*) A book.

JOHN: I'll be careful, and quiet.

JOE: All right. Go on. Go on.

JOHN: Thank you—thank you—
(*He goes round the turn in the stair.* JOE *looks up at him, alone
again with his assorted animals.*)

6. ZION CHAPEL. WELSH VILLAGE
Earlier that morning.
  *The Preacher, whose voice we heard over the wet streets at the
beginning, finishes reading the chapter from Genesis from a huge Bible.*

PREACHER: (*With sonorous self-satisfaction*) And all the flesh died
that moved upon the earth, both of fowl and of cattle and of
beast and of every creeping thing that creepeth upon the
earth, and every man. All in whose nostrils was the breath
of life, of all that was in the dry land died. And every living
substance was destroyed which was upon the face of the
ground, both man and cattle and the creeping things and
the fowl of the heavens; and they were destroyed from the
earth: and Noah only remained alive, and they that are
with him in the ark.
(*He shuts the big book with a sombre relish.*)
And Noah only remained alive and they that were with him
in the ark!
(*Pause. He glares at the congregation.*)
Are we any *less* wicked, any *less* violent, any *less* corrupt
today? Can we learn anything *at all* from the story of that
just man, Noah?
(*Pause. We see* JOE *in congregation. Then, a banal, preacher's
touch.*)
What is the long-range weather forecast, brethren? (*Slight
pause.*) A sermon then, is it?
(*He takes off his spectacles, in no great hurry.*)
It's easy to write and even easier to deliver a sermon, you
know. Too easy. If I've learned anything, I've learned *that!*
I used to *list–en* to myself as a young man up here in this
fine oak pulpit. (*Smacks it affectionately.*) And I used to *love*
what it was I heard.
(*He scowls down at them.*)
That was a joke, see!
(*They laugh, dutifully. But he neatly catches the laugh on the rise.*)
But the *filth* in our *hearts* is no joke!
(*An abrupt silence.*)
You will remember that when the waters subsided and
Noah built an altar unto the Lord, the Lord said in his
heart—'I will not again curse the ground any more for
man's sake—for the imagination of man's heart is evil from
his youth.'

(*Pick up* JOE, *disturbed.*)
So the answer to my question is—No! No. We are not any
less corrupt, any less violent, any less wicked than many
before the great flood. So don't congratulate yourself. But
God has made us this specific promise, a promise renewed
with every rainbow. *He* will not smite all living creatures.
'While the earth remaineth,' it says, 'while the earth
remaineth, seedtime and harvest, and cold and heat, and
summer and winter, and day and night shall not cease.' But
we are, while on this good earth, incapable of seeing the
breath of life for what it really is. 'The imagination of man's
heart is evil from his youth.' And that is what the rainbow
says also! We are none of us good enough for this earth. We
all of us lack the holy imagination that could see life as the
thrilling wondrous gift that it really is.
(JOE *can be seen battling with something new inside himself.*)

JOE: (*Shouts, stands*) No! That's not true! Not true!
(*Consternation. Such a thing has never happened before. The*
PREACHER *gapes, wordless.* JOE *pushes, storms his way along the*
row. Everyone is very embarrassed.)
(*In aisle, furious*) You've *had* your life, Daniel. You've lived
it. You've got no right—no right at all—
(*But he cannot speak clearly. He stares wildly at the* PREACHER,
then dashes towards the door at the back. An awkward, tense
silence.)

PREACHER: (*Shaken, humiliated*) We will—yes—pardon me a
moment—we will sing hymn number 307 in *Sankey's Sacred*
Songs and Solos. (*Tremble*) God is here, and that to bless us
with the Spirit's quickening power. See, the cloud already
bending Waits to drop the grateful— (*His voice breaks*)
—sh–shower—
(*As the harmonium swells and feet scrape, the* PREACHER *turns his*
head aside, deeply upset.)

7. LUCY'S BEDROOM ABOVE THE SHOP

Dusk.

JOHN *shuts the door behind him, over-careful.*

The room is poorly lit, because the curtains are closed.

LUCY *stirs, propped up on her pillows.*

JOHN: (*Half whisper*) Lucy?

(*Slight pause.*)

LUCY: Bobby? Is that you, Bobby?

JOHN: Bobby? Who— No it's me. John.

(*He moves to the bed.*)

LUCY: Oh. John. Yes. Hello.

(*But she cannot keep the disappointment out of her voice.*)

JOHN: Shall I put the light on?

LUCY: The switch is by the door.

JOHN: Who is Bobby?

(*Click: light.*)

LUCY: (*Blink*) Ouch!

JOHN: Is it too bright?

LUCY: No, no. (*Smile.*) Hello, John. This is a nice surprise.

JOHN: I hitched down. I— it was pouring all the way.

LUCY: You look a bit bedraggled.

JOHN: (*Nervous*) I simply *had* to see you. I've been longing to see you.

LUCY: Sit down, John.

(*He sits. And stares at her.*)

JOHN: How are—I mean, is it—bad? Do you feel—

LUCY: Tired. Mostly tired.

JOHN: Yes. Of course.

(*Awkward, sickroom pause.*)

LUCY: (*Smile*) If I was you I wouldn't visit you if you were me.

JOHN: That sounds more Irish than Welsh.

LUCY: Celtic, anyway.

(*Another awkward little pause.*)

JOHN: I've brought you a present.

(*He attacks his bag.*)

LUCY: Not grapes, I hope.

JOHN: No, not quite so squashy—a book—

(*He holds out a fat book.* Wordsworth's Hawkshead *by T. W. Thompson, as though it were, somehow, more than a book.*)

LUCY: But John—it's—look at it—as fat as an old Bible—

JOHN: You can dip into it Lucy. It's full of stuff—I think you'll like it and—hope so—

LUCY: Of course I will. Thank you. It's very nice.

(*But she makes no attempt to take it.*)

JOHN: (*Half offering it*) This old man—Thompson—he spent *sixty years* writing it—or sixty years gathering together all the tiniest bits and pieces about Wordsworth's childhood.

LUCY: Goodness.

(*But she doesn't sound thrilled. Tiny pause.*)

JOHN: (*Helplessly*) It even finds out exactly what sort of cakes Wordsworth had for tea.

(*He lets out a nervous, twitchy little laugh.*)

LUCY: Sounds like an obsession.

JOHN: In a way, yes. I suppose it does.

LUCY: Oh, well. At least he got it published in the end.

JOHN: After his death, yes.

(*They both laugh. They both fall silent.*)

LUCY: Put it on the table, John.

(*He is disappointed that she does not take it.*)

JOHN: I've—yes—here then. (*Putting it down*) I've written inside it.

LUCY: What—the recipe, I suppose?

JOHN: Recipe?

LUCY: For the tea cakes.

(*He is hurt, the wet lad.*)

Oh, John—no—I'm sorry. It's a lovely thing to do.

JOHN: I made it Wordsworth because—do you remember our first walk?

LUCY: By the river. Yes.

JOHN: I'll never forget it. You were—

LUCY: Unforgettable, it seems.

(*Slight pause.*)

JOHN: (*Uncomfortable*) No, you were going on a bit about Wordsworth and Coleridge, the weird way they regarded

each other and so on—
LUCY: I don't care about that sort of detail any more.
JOHN: But— No?
LUCY: It's quite a relief, really.
(*She smiles.*)
JOHN: (*Quietly*) What *do* you care about, Lucy? (*Pause.*) What do
you care about?
(*No answer—he gets up.*)
LUCY: The way carrots taste different from cabbage.
JOHN: Oh.
LUCY: (*Laugh*) Don't be so disappointed!
JOHN: No, I remember you talking about Wordsworth, that's all.
You sat down under that tree. A copper beech or something.
LUCY: *Fell* down! You walk like *they* used to walk—
JOHN: Who used to walk?
LUCY: Wordsworth and Coleridge.
JOHN: Oh, yes. Well—I do stride out a bit. Anyone would think
I was getting somewhere, wouldn't they?
LUCY: Loping along—and talking all the time!
JOHN: I was—nervous.
(*She sighs, irritated.*)
I've missed you a lot. I keep thinking about you.
LUCY: So do I.
JOHN: (*Brightening*) Really? — Oh Lucy—you—
LUCY: Keep thinking about me, I mean.
JOHN: Oh.
(*She laughs.*)
LUCY: When Edward VII was dying—his last words, so they
say—were absolutely splendid. Some idiot no doubt
suggested he would soon be fit enough to recuperate at
Bognor Regis. And he said—do you know what he said?
JOHN: Lucy . . .
LUCY: 'Bugger Bognor.' That's what he said. 'Bugger Bognor.'
(*Impulsively he grabs hold of her hand.*)
JOHN: I've—missed you, really missed you.
LUCY: We only went out three or four times, John.
JOHN: And I wrote to you, here. A long letter.

LUCY: Yes.

JOHN: You—um—you didn't reply. Was it that silly, my letter?

LUCY: (*Evasive*) I don't like answering letters. I can't now,
anyway. Too difficult.

(*Pause.*)

JOHN: (*Soft*) Your hand is hot.

LUCY: I took out life membership of the Oxford Society last year.
Do you think I can claim a rebate?

JOHN: Oh, Lucy. Please!

LUCY: (*Laugh*) Bugger Bognor. Or, in this case—

JOHN: (*Passionately*) Please! There are so many things I'd like to
say to you.

LUCY: What sort of things?

JOHN: Real things. The things that I feel.

LUCY: And that will make you feel good, will it?

JOHN: (*Shocked*) Lucy . . . no . . .

LUCY: Make you feel better—mmm?

JOHN: No—listen, please—I'm not trying to—no, I've been
thinking so much, such a lot about you that I just suddenly
decided to come down here and spill it out, spill it all out.
Lucy?

LUCY: Spill out what? *Blood?*

JOHN: No. What I feel about y—

LUCY: Oh, words. You mean *words*. Spill out *words?*

JOHN: Well—no—yes—I mean I want to explain to you what I
feel and think about you and hope for you and—and—

(*He shrugs, helpless, inarticulate.*)

LUCY: Piss off, John.

JOHN: (*Astounded*) Pardon?

(*Silence. She lies back, eyes half-closed, exhausted.*)

(*Whisper*) Lucy?

(*Silence. He stares at her, hurt and scared.*)

(*Upset*) I—yes, I'll come up and see you a bit later. I'll go
down and talk to your father—

(*She looks at him.*)

LUCY: Did he seem all right to you? Normal, I mean. Whatever
that is.

JOHN: (*Hesitant*) He—well—

LUCY: (*Interrupting*) His Christianity survived the death of my
mother and the defection of my brother, but not *this*, I
think. He was very strange when he came back from Zion
this morning. Angry—or ashamed—

JOHN: Zion—?

LUCY: The Chapel. Up the road.

JOHN: Oh. Yes. He—well he did seem upset by the sermon or
something.

LUCY: Oh, God. I could see it coming. Christ, how boring!

JOHN: Perhaps he feels—well—

LUCY: My brother—he— (*laughs*) —when he gets bad service in
a shop or a restaurant he shouts at the top of his voice, 'I'll
have you know I'm a shareholder in this company!' But it
isn't quite so effective to rise up and shake your fist at God
though, is it?

JOHN: (*Blank*) God. No.

LUCY: Ask him about the animals. He loves those. Take his
mind off it.

JOHN: (*Brightening*) Then you don't mind if I stay a little
while?

LUCY: But it's term time, isn't it?

JOHN: Oh. Bugger Bognor.
(*She laughs, more affectionate.*)

LUCY: Thanks, John. I *am* glad to see you, you know.

JOHN: Didn't seem like it!

LUCY: Do something for me, will you?

JOHN: (*Extravagantly*) Anything!
(*She looks at him.*)
I mean, if I can.

LUCY: Make Dad write to Bobby.

JOHN: Bobby?

LUCY: My brother. I want to see him before—I want to see him
very, very much. He's the nicest person I ever knew.

JOHN: Where is he?

LUCY: Where? Oh—bleeding to death in front of some leery,
beer-swilling stag party, I expect. Make my father get in

touch with him. Will you?

JOHN: Y–yes.

LUCY: And if he won't, *you* do it. There's a forwarding address in the left-hand drawer of the kitchen cabinet.

JOHN: OK.

LUCY: (*Insistent*) I want to see him.

JOHN: Yes. All right.

LUCY: Good.

(*Pause.*)

JOHN: Lucy—?

LUCY: No, John. I'm—tired. Go downstairs.

JOHN: Can't I just sit here?

LUCY: No. I want to break wind.

(*His face a comic mixture of embarrassment, and even disillusion, he gets up quickly.*)

JOHN: Oh. S–sorry—yes. I'll— Yes. I'll come up again—

(*He backs out of the room.*)

8. ZION CHAPEL

The congregation belts out the chorus of the hymn the Preacher announced, No.307, Sankey, in real, Revivalist fervour.

CHAPEL CONGREGATION: (*Sing*)

Let it come . . . O Lord we pray Thee!

Let the shower . . . of bless–ing fall

We are wait–ing . . . we are wait–ing

Oh revive . . . the hearts of all!

9. THE PET SHOP

Evening.

Some powdered water fleas float down into the water of a large glass tank of brilliantly coloured and teeming little neon tetra fish.

JOE is feeding his stock. As he works, he is half talking to himself, quietly, disjointedly.

JOE: (*To fish*) Sick of you lot—never say a word—gollup, gollup—greed–y— Get some mirror carps—no, cichlids. I'll get some cichlids and put them in with you. Soon eat you lot up! Tcha!

(*He stops. And puts his face up against the tank, staring at the swirling fish. Silence.*)

(*Murmur*) Fish. Fish. What do *you* care? What do *you* know?

(*He suddenly slaps the side of the tank, angrily. The fish swirl away. Making strange whimpering noises, he moves across the shop, feeding other animals.*)

(*To rabbit*) And you don't know, boyo. You don't know. Why? Why? Why?

(*He puts water in hamster's cage. And feeds mice with chopped carrot, bread and birdseed.*)

Eat and sleep. Eat and sleep. That's all there is. Day in day— Eat and sleep and die. Pointless. All— (*almost spits*) —pointless.

(*The big cockatoo shrieks.* JOE *moves across and stands in front of it.*)

(*Evenly*) Lis–ten you. I give you fair warning. I've *told* you to stop your rack–et. You're as stupid a creature as ever sat on a perch and—

(*He stops. Leans elbows on counter, and stares at the bird. The bird seems to stare back, beadily.*)

(*Soft*) She's not going to leave us, is she? Eh? No–o–o.

(*Animal sounds from shop, excited by feeding ritual.*)

(*Flat*) Eat and sleep and die. Eat and sleep and die. Is that what it's all for?

(*The bird squawks again.*)

Ach! Shut up! You've never got anything bright to say! Great noisy fool!

(*As he turns away in disgust, the shop door bangs. Muttering incoherently,* JOE *goes across and unbolts the door. The* PREACHER *is standing on the step. It is still raining.*)

10. ON PET SHOP DOORSTEP

PREACHER: Good evening, Mr Jones.

    (*Fractional pause.*)

JOE: (*Formal*) Good evening, Mr Watkins.

    (*They look at each other.*)

PREACHER: There's wet it is, Joe.

JOE: Indeed it is, Daniel. Very wet.

(*They examine each other again.*)

PREACHER: You didn't come to evening service, then.

JOE: No. I didn't come.

(*Pause.*)

PREACHER: Even so, Joe—no need to keep a man on the step in weather like this, now.

(JOE *hesitates slightly, then behaves properly.*)

JOE: No, quite right. Quite right. I'm very sorry, Mr Watkins.

(*He beckons the* PREACHER *in, and shuts the door.*)

11. THE PET SHOP

The PREACHER *stands in the middle of the shop, looking round, sniffing slightly.*

PREACHER: Animals. They do have their distinct smells, Joe.

(JOE *is on the brink of hostility.*)

JOE: Don't notice any more.

(*The* PREACHER *feels awkward.*)

PREACHER: I've got some cold lamb for my supper. So I shan't be long about. It's just that—

JOE: Lamb—eh.

PREACHER: (*Chuckles*) I like to go from the lamb of God straight to the lamb of Cledwynn James. Eh, Joe?

JOE: Good Welsh lamb.

PREACHER: Finest in the world. Sweet, see.

(*Pause.*)

JOE: (*Almost aggressive*) Well, it's feed time for this lot, too. So unless there was something spec–if–ic—

PREACHER: (*Quickly*) Can I sit down, Joe?

(*He plumps himself on the stool before* JOE *can say otherwise.*)

JOE: (*With a glint*) There now, and I spilled some dried water fleas on that stool.

(*The* PREACHER *almost jumps up.*)

PREACHER (*Controlling himself*) No harm. No harm.

JOE: I don't think I shall be carrying on with the Chapel, Mr Watkins.

PREACHER: Oh, now. There's sorry I am to hear it, bach.

Joe's Ark

JOE: Nothing personal, you understand.

PREACHER: Joe—

JOE: I've got a lot of work on my hands as it is. And—

PREACHER: Don't decide too hasty. Think on it a bit more, eh?

JOE: Mind you, I should have waited until Chapel was over. Caused a bit of comment, no doubt.

PREACHER: There's something about a pulpit brings out—the showman or something like that in the best and the worst of preachers. I wasn't thinking at all at the time of your distress. (*Hard to say*) I'm sorry, Joe. I'm very sorry.

JOE: No need to be. Either the Bible is true or it isn't. You cannot add to it, nor take away.

PREACHER: I'm not apologizing for the Bible. God forbid! No— but there's many another word in that Book which would have done better this morning.

(*Pause.*)

JOE: (*Almost a cry*) There's no sense in it, Dan. No sense in it!

PREACHER: No sense *we* can see, perhaps.

(JOE *is now walking up and down the shop floor, agitated. Animals in shot. The* PREACHER *watches him, concerned, careful.*)

JOE: No sense—no sense at all—no sense in anything— anywhere—no—none—*none!*

PREACHER: Joe—listen a minute . . .

(JOE *moves around attending to the animals.*)

JOE: (*Snarl*) Rain! Rain!

PREACHER: Beg pardon?

JOE: Let it all happen again, and the sooner the better!

PREACHER: Joe? What are you on about, man?

JOE: If Lucy is going to be taken, then—

(*He flaps his arms, just once, and falls silent.*)

PREACHER: It's almost too hard to bear, I know. But God— He calls the good to himself—

(*Almost before he can get it out,* JOE *thrusts his face into the* PREACHER*'s face.*)

JOE: (*Hiss*) What—did—you—say?

PREACHER: God calls the good—to—to heaven. Joe?

JOE: Then what *you* doing here?

108

PREACHER: Talking to you, you mean?

JOE: No! On earth! What are you doing still alive and chomping and chewing your cold lamb and stale words!

(*Pause.*)

PREACHER: No call for that, mun.

JOE: It's words like that which stick in my craw! I don't want to hear it! I don't want it! *Do you understand?*

PREACHER: (*Dully*) Yes.

JOE: Ach! Two terms at Oxford. Then—

(*Silence.*)

PREACHER: A scholar. A real scholar, Joe.

(JOE *stares at him, almost with hatred.*)

JOE: Scholar?

PREACHER: When she was at the Sunday School she knew words, long words, which even Miss Thomas couldn't quite pick up . . .

JOE: Osteogenic-carcinoma.

PREACHER: Pardon?

(JOE *spits out each syllable.*)

JOE: Ost–e–o–genic–car–cin–o–ma!

(*Pause.*)

PREACHER: (*Uncomfortable*) Is that what it's called, Joe? This—ah— (*Almost whispers the word*) —cancer?

JOE: That's it! That's your love of God for you!

PREACHER: (*With difficulty*) We shall have to—we must pray for her . . .

JOE: Ost–e–o–gen–ic–car–cin–o–ma!

(*The* PREACHER *shifts uncomfortably.*)

PREACHER: Do you believe in God, Joe? Do you still believe?

(*No answer.*)

The question doesn't really mean very much except when you are in a terrible crisis. Joe?

JOE: (*Shout*) There's no sense in it!

(*The* PREACHER *lowers his eyes.*)

PREACHER: Look around you . . . just look around . . .

JOE: (*Abrupt*) Don't let your cold lamb get too dry on the plate, Daniel. Pity to spoil it.

PREACHER: The answer has got to be here—got to be in front of you—or nowhere.

JOE: What do you mean? What answer!

PREACHER: All these animals. Look at them. All these different creatures. So beautifully fashioned and designed, Joe.

JOE: For sale. All for sale.

PREACHER: Oh, aye. For sale, yes. What are those pretty things over there?

JOE: What—these?

PREACHER: Yes—incredibly beautiful, they are. Unimaginable.

(JOE *purses his lips, just a tiny bit pleased.*)

JOE: Neon tetras, these.

PREACHER: No painter could do that, see.

(*They both look at the fish tank for a moment. Then* JOE *turns away.*)

JOE: That's got nothing to d—

PREACHER: (*Quickly*) They don't know anything about anything beyond the water in their tank.

JOE: And the heating element.

PREACHER: Ah, yes. Tropical, yes.

JOE: If I put a cichlid in among them, though.

PREACHER: Another sort of fish, would that be?

JOE: Another sort of fish, Mr Watkins.

(*Pause.*)

PREACHER: Eat them, would it?

JOE: From tail to mouth, whole.

(*Pause.*)

PREACHER: All I know, there *has* to be a pattern. An overall purpose. Otherwise—

JOE: (*With relish*) Gobble them up in two seconds flat. Snap! Swallow!

PREACHER: I suppose everything's kept in a—a—well, a sort of *balance*. Has to be.

JOE: That depends on me in here, doesn't it?

PREACHER: How do you mean?

JOE: One cichlid in with that little lot—nasty!

PREACHER: But you wouldn't do it, though. Not for the sake of it.

JOE: Or switch off their heating element. Easy. Or starve that

bird over there—how about that, then? Stop him
squawking, won't it!

PREACHER: No, no. You are not a cruel man.

JOE: No! And if I was God, see, I wouldn't do what *He*'s doing to
our Lucy!

PREACHER: (*Doggedly*) Either Almighty God is merciful, or there is
no God.

JOE: Then there is no God!
(*Pause.*)

PREACHER: Look at all of them—bird, fishes, rabbit . . .

JOE: No, Dan, no—

PREACHER: . . . all the animals, all different bones, all different
colours and shapes, different brains, different habits, food,
noises, smells—how can you say there's no sense? No pattern?

JOE: Chapel is over, Mr Watkins.

PREACHER: (*Emotional*) We shall all die, Joe. Like all these animals.
We all have our cycle. Our time.

JOE: Not a young girl! *That*'s not right! That can *never* be right!

PREACHER: How do we *know*, Joe? How do w—

JOE: Go home, Dan.

PREACHER: Pardon?

JOE: Go home, mun. Go and chew up your nice bit of lamb.
(*Pause.*)

PREACHER: (*Sigh*) Yes. (*Stands.*) Mary doesn't like me to be late.
(*He stands awkward and distressed in the middle of the shop.*)
Joe—I'm not much use, I know, but I just wanted to say—
(JOE *stares at him.*)

JOE: (*Interrupting*) Mint sauce, too.

PREACHER: Mint?

JOE: Can't have lamb without some nice fresh mint, Daniel.

PREACHER: True. Very true.
(*He goes to the door, shoulders drooping.*)

JOE: Mind the step.

PREACHER: Even Our Lord in his greatest agony thought that God
His Father had forsaken him—

JOE: (*Holding door*) There's a big puddle on the pavement here. Go
careful.

111

PREACHER: (*Going out*) Pray, Joe! Pray!

JOE: Good night, Mr Watkins. Enjoy your supper.

PREACHER: (*Over shoulder*) Good night, Mr Jones.

(JOE *shuts the door. Stands facing it a moment. Then hurls it open and rushes out.*)

12. PAVEMENT OUTSIDE SHOP

The PREACHER *is slowly walking away, shoulders drooping, seemingly oblivious of the still falling rain.*

JOE, *coming out, glares at the departing, darkening figure.*

JOE: (*Shout*) And perhaps Our Lord was forsaken! Perhaps he *was*— have you thought of that!

(*The* PREACHER *plods on, his back to us.*)

(*Furious*) No answer, eh! No answer!

(*He looks about him, at the wet and dark street, and retreats back into the shop.*)

13. THE PET SHOP

JOE *comes back in, disturbed by what he has just shouted. He looks at his animals, one at a time. They seem to look back, strange, lost.*

Suddenly JOE *lets out a low moan and sinks down in prayer, speaking the way he spoke as a boy, in that strange, moving, beleaguered tongue of his childhood.*

JOE: Ni wyddwn beth a ddywedwn, annwyl Iesu. Tystiaf am dy ddioddefaint ar groes Calfaria. Paid ag anghofio tristwch y dioddefaint hyn, annwyl Iesu. Edrych arnaf fi yn Dy drugaredd a chofia fy ngeneth fach sydd mewn poen a blinder. Erfynaf arnat fel yr erfyniast Ti ar y Tad.

Paid â gadael iddi farw, ni allwn ddal y boen. Cymer fi a'r hyn oll sydd gennyf yn ei lle, ie, cymer fi, a gad i'r eneth fach gael byw.*

---

*More prosaic: I didn't know what I was saying, dear Jesus Christ. I know how you suffered, hanging up there nailed to the wood. All I ask is that you remember that awful pain, dear Jesus, my Jesus, and look down in pity on me and on my little girl, for surely we too are in agony. We call out to you as you called out to Your Father! Please, please do not let it happen. Please. Take me instead, and all my animals. Take me and let her live!

14. LUCY'S BEDROOM
Night.

    JOHN *and* LUCY.
JOHN: (*Earnest*) But *why* do you want me to go back, Lucy. Why?
LUCY: (*Weaker*) John—listen—
JOHN: I must stay with you! I must!
LUCY: (*Half laugh*) There's no future in it.
JOHN: You *are* my future, Lucy!
LUCY: Think about what you are saying.
    (*He grips at her hand.*)
JOHN: I *know* what I'm saying!
LUCY: (*Quietly*) Let go of my hand.
JOHN: Lucy. Lucy—
LUCY: (*Rising tone*) Let go of my hand, please.
    (*Fractional pause. Then he lets go of her hand.*)
JOHN: But you must know how, must know how I—
    (*She turns her head away.*)
LUCY: (*Mumble*) No future in it.
JOHN: I can't hear you. What? What is it?
LUCY: I can't *live* inside *your* head.
JOHN: (*Stupidly*) You won't die there, either!
LUCY: (*Barely audible*) Shit.
JOHN: I love you!
LUCY: (*Faint, but satiric*) You love me?
JOHN: Yes. I do.
    (*Pause.*)
LUCY: (*Very faint*) Proust.
JOHN: Pardon?
LUCY: There's an aunt or something—
JOHN: (*Bewildered*) Proust?
LUCY: (*Stronger*) . . . who wants her relatives to die in a fire so
    that she can grieve for them without having the
    responsibilities of a *real*—a *real*—commitment.
    (*A hurt silence. She stares up at the ceiling.*)
JOHN: That's not—that's now how it is at all.
LUCY: No?
    (*She winces in a physical pain he doesn't even notice.*)

JOHN: No!
(*Pause. She composes herself.*)
LUCY: So I— (*Slight gasp*) —so I *can't die*—in your head.
JOHN: I'm saying that you will always—
LUCY: Live. In your head.
JOHN: (*Struggling*) I'm saying that—that—
LUCY: Words. C–Counters in a game.
JOHN: (*Simply*) I just want to be with you. As long as I can.
(*Silence.*)
Sh–Shall I—um—shall I read to you? Lucy?
(*She closes her eyes. He shifts uneasily.*)
I've written to your brother. I'll post it in the morning.
(*She opens her eyes.*)
Lucy?
LUCY: (*Weary*) Good. That's good.
(*He frowns with an unbidden pang of jealousy.*)

15. A SQUALID, CRAMPED LITTLE DRESSING ROOM
Night.
The big face shining under the naked bulb in the mirror is that of lewd comedian BOBBY, *removing his make-up. He bares his teeth at himself. Then relaxes his face, losing the horrible sniggery semi-permanent leer of his stage performance.*
COMEDIAN: God! I need some new material.
(*Pull out to show* SALLY *flopped half-naked in the lone armchair.*)
SALLY: We could always have it off on stage, I suppose.
(*He whirls round.*)
COMEDIAN: Shut up, Sally!
SALLY: Wouldn't be much worse than some of these stinking jokes.
COMEDIAN: It's all they want. It's all they'll ever want. The pigs.
SALLY: That—and me coming on with my tits hanging out to bring it all to (*Mimics*) a *taystful* conclusion.
COMEDIAN: Sally—?
SALLY: I feel like—
COMEDIAN: (*Quickly*) Don't Sal! Don't!
SALLY: No! I feel a right tart stuck up there while you dribble on

114

about 'the hills and dales'. Might just as well be one.
(*He looks at her carefully.*)

COMEDIAN: It's a living.

SALLY: (*Contemptuously*) A living!

COMEDIAN: (*Mock cackle*) Yeh—a living death!
(*Silence.*)

SALLY: Yes. You do need some new material, Bobby.

COMEDIAN: There was this man walking down the road with a
hippopotamus, see, and—
(*He stops and looks at himself in the mirror.*)

SALLY: Forget it.

COMEDIAN: Well, that's one thing my bloody Da never had!

SALLY: What is?

COMEDIAN: A hippopotamus. (*Sniff.*) Plenty of hypocrisy but
never a hippopotamus. Canting old fool!

SALLY: Bobby.

COMEDIAN: Bluebottle maggots and the Bible. There's a healthy
combination for you, eh?

SALLY: Almost as good as what we've got going for us now.
(*Moody silence.*)

COMEDIAN: OK. Let's go and eat.

SALLY: Where?

COMEDIAN: Bound to be somewhere open. Even in this
dump.

SALLY: A fish and chip shop if we're lucky.

COMEDIAN: Sally—listen—

SALLY: (*Bitterly*) Oh shut up!
(*He looks at himself in the mirror again.*)

COMEDIAN: Tortoises and terrapins. Hamsters and rabbits.
Alligators and skinks.

SALLY: What are you talking about!

COMEDIAN: (*Snigger*) Goldfish on toast.

SALLY: Ugh.

COMEDIAN: He beat hell out of me once. I fried some of his
bleedin' fish.

SALLY: Give me a cigarette.
(*He throws a packet across.*)

COMEDIAN: (*Still looking at himself*) My face is getting set in a
    sort of—leer.

SALLY: Light?

COMEDIAN: Yep. A sort of permanent—leer.

SALLY: (*Fed up*) Have you got a light?

COMEDIAN: Get up and light it yourself!

SALLY: (*Mockingly*) Oooo!

COMEDIAN: And get some clothes on, you bloody slut!

    (*With a slow, deliberately exaggerated obscenity, she wags two
    fingers at him, unlit cigarette drooping in her mouth. It looks, at this
    moment, as though they hate each other.*)

16. LUCY'S BEDROOM

*LUCY stirs in response to a tuneless drunken bellow from a lone reveller in
street below, which is receding. She stares up at the ceiling. The voice
fades away. Silence. Her clock tick–tocks.*

LUCY: Bugger Bognor. (*Pause.*) Buggerbognorbuggerbognor
    buggerbognor. Bugger!

17. PET SHOP

*Poor light. Gradually we discern JOE in the corner, on his stool, alone.
Faint animal noises. Then the door at the back clicks open, sending a shaft
of light across JOE's face.*

JOHN: (*Soft*) Mr Jones—?

    (*JOE does not reply. Uncertain, JOHN pads into the room.*)

    Why are you sitting in here?

    (*No reply.*)

    Sh–Shall I put the light on?

    (*No reply.*)

    Mr Jones?

JOE: No.

    (*Pause.*)

JOHN: Are you—all right? Would you like me to make a cup of
    tea?

    (*No reply.*)

    C–Can I *talk* to you?

JOE: Go back to bed.

JOHN: I'd like to talk to you. Please.

JOE: I can't stop you.

JOHN: (*Nervously*) It would be nice to have some light though—

JOE: No!

JOHN: All right.

JOE: (*Not looking at him*) Don't need to see to speak. And you don't need to speak to see.

JOHN: Pardon?

JOE: Think about it.

(*Pause.*)

JOHN: Yes.

JOE: Well—what do you want then?

JOHN: Are you—are you going to sit down here all night?

JOE: Mind your own.

JOHN: Sorry.

JOE: (*Partly apologetic*) It's better to sit with the animals. Sometimes.

JOHN: I suppose you get fond of them.

JOE: (*Bitter*) Oh, aye. I'm their God, see.

(*Pause.*)

You'll be going back tomorrow, then?

JOHN: (*Hesitant*) Well—I—

JOE: (*Swift*) You can't stay here.

JOHN: Why not?

(*One of the animals makes a noise.*)

JOE: Shut up!

JOHN: The smell, too. All these animals. But she loves them—doesn't she? Wants to come down and feed them.

JOE: (*With a sudden eagerness*) Was she happy there? Was it like all she hoped it was?

JOHN: Oxford?

JOE: When Miss Thomas first put the idea in her head—oh, when she was 15 and a bit I suppose—Lucy couldn't help standing by the signpost up by the Miners' Welfare. Stand there sometimes and look at it. The one to the A40. Second name from the bottom of it was Oxford, see. Oxford.

JOHN: She—yes, I think so. She seemed to—glow there. Yes.

117

JOHN: Glow?

JOHN: Words—ideas—all that—you know—

JOE: (*Flat*) Words.

> (*Pause.*)

JOHN: Why don't we put the light on?

JOE: No.

> (*Pause.*)

JOHN: She—I know it would make her happy if you made your son welcome here.

JOE: (*Angry*) That's nothing to do with you, is it? That's family.

JOHN: I know. I'm sorry. But she wants to see him.

JOE: He near nigh broke his mother's heart, that boy. And—yes. I know.

JOHN: She wants to see him very much.

> (*Pause.* JOE *struggles.*)

JOE: I'll write.

JOHN: I beg your pardon, Mr Jones. But I—well, I've already done it. She asked me to. And—

> (*Pause.*)

JOE: English. Aren't you?

JOHN: Y–Yes.

JOE: Thought so. No manners.

JOHN: I'm sorry.

JOE: Family is family down here, see. We don't go poking our noses into family. Not your place, is it?

JOHN: No.

> (*Silence.*)

JOE: Did she go in a punt? On the river—all that sort of thing?

JOHN: Yes.

JOE: In her long black gown?

JOHN: (*Hesitant*) Well—

JOE: Her scholar's gown.

JOHN: (*To please him*) Yes.

> (*Pause.*)

JOE: You didn't mess her about or anything like that?

JOHN: Pardon?

JOE: Spoil her!

JOHN: N–No.

JOE: She was a good girl, see. Always was. A very good girl.

JOHN: (*Sob*) Was?

JOE: (*Shocked*) Was? I didn't say was! She's not going to—

JOHN: (*Crying*) Please—why—please Mr Jo—

JOE: Shut up! Shut up!

(*But* JOHN *is crying easily now.*)

JOHN: I—I—sorry . . .

JOE: (*Angry*) Put the light on then. Put the light on you great baby!

JOHN: No!

(*He cries hard, but perhaps with a hint of enjoyable self-pity.*)

JOE: No sense in sitting here in dark.

(*But they keep their positions.* JOHN's *sobs subside.*)

I'll make a cup of tea in a minute. Nice cup of tea. In a minute.

18. A FAST-FOOD BAR

Morning.

Brightly tatty, with tinned music drifting about.

BOBBY, *the* COMEDIAN, *is eating—and reading, rereading a note he has propped up against a sauce bottle. His face heavy.*

Behind and at an angle to him a slim PAKISTANI *is sweeping up accumulated muck from under the bolted-down tables and chairs.*

COMEDIAN: (*Mutter*) Can't be true . . . can't be . . . can't . . .

(*The* PAKISTANI's *broad broom pushes the pile of mess nearer. The sweeper seems dreamily absorbed in his menial task. Music, hard, bright, tatty.* COMEDIAN *puts a lump of hamburger into his mouth, chews slowly, folds up note. Then catches sight of* PAKISTANI.)

Hey! Stop it—

(*The* PAKISTANI *looks at him, expressionless, arm still slowly pushing, dream-like.*)

(*Swallow.*) Stop it! Bloody hell! Stop doing that will ya! I'm eating.

(*Spasm of confusion on* PAKISTANI's *face. He grips his broom tightly, staring back at the suddenly enraged* COMEDIAN.)

PAKISTANI: Please?

119

Joe's Ark

(*The* COMEDIAN *throws his knife down on the plate with an almost operatic gesture. His rage, of course, is about the news in the letter.*)

COMEDIAN: God Almighty!

PAKISTANI: Please?

COMEDIAN: You shouldn't sweep all that shit in front of anybody when they're eating!

(*The* PAKISTANI, *marooned, looks across for help to a* MAN *in chef's cap at the 'griddle'.*)

(*Stoking his rage*) Cigarette ends—lumps of meat—all that muck—what the flaming bloody hell—!

(*The* PAKISTANI *shrugs and carries on sweeping, puzzled.*)

(*Yell*) Stop it! Stop it you dirty pig!

(*So loud that everybody stops chewing. The* CHEF *sighs, starts to come forward.*)

And I'm not finishing *this*!

(*The* COMEDIAN *pushes his plate away in ferocious clatter.*)

PAKISTANI: (*Worried*) No—no understand—

COMEDIAN: I'm not paying for it neither!

(*The* CHEF *pads forward.*)

CHEF: What's all the trouble here . . .

(*Rising, flushed, the* COMEDIAN *points to the floor-sweepings.*)

COMEDIAN: Look! Look at all that shit!

CHEF: Now, now—look here, sir—

COMEDIAN: And he can fucking well sweep that up with all the other bloody mess!

(*Throws his food on the floor. Register other faces, half delighted, half appalled.*)

CHEF: There's no call for that—none at all—!

COMEDIAN: No? What about that then! Can I do that?

(*Picks up a sticky sauce bottle and glugs some out on to the floor.*)

CHEF: You're off your nut, mate! You don't treat good food like that!

COMEDIAN: (*Quivering*) I came in here to *eat* not be sick!

CHEF: (*Retreating to officiousness*) And you've eaten some of it, sir, so you can pay for—

COMEDIAN: Bloody rubbish pushed in front of you when you're eating—

CHEF: You can't do it. Ripping up your bill. You just can't do it.
COMEDIAN: (*Spluttering*) What am I? A pig? A pig—or what?
CHEF: (*Adamant*) Double burger and chips.
COMEDIAN: Stuff it! You can stuff it!
   (*He pushes the* CHEF *aside and storms towards glass door that opens on to pavement.*)
CHEF: Hey! Come back—you can't—
   (*The* COMEDIAN *stops at door, glowering, maddened.*)
COMEDIAN: Put bluebottle maggots on the menu, you dirty sods! Tinned maggots!
   (*He sweeps out. The* CHEF *and the* PAKISTANI *look at each other.*)
CHEF: (*Snarl*) What you do that for, nig nog!
PAKISTANI: (*Blink*) Please?
   (*The* COMEDIAN *pushes in again from the street, wild eyed with grief, holding glass door half open.*)
COMEDIAN: (*Bellow*) Furthermore, I'll have you know I'm a shareholder in this company! And I shall do something about it!
   (*Bangs door shut and stalks off ridiculously. Momentary pause—then the biggest laugh of his life.*)

19. LUCY'S BEDROOM
Day.

   JOE *stands with a tray at the side of her bed. But she is asleep, beads of sweat on her forehead.*
JOE: (*Uncertain*) Lucy?
   (*She does not stir. He looks at her, a long look.*)
   (*Soft*) Lucy?
   (*She still sleeps. He sits beside her.*)
   (*Whisper*) Oh I wish I could tell you what you are to me, my baby.
   (*Silence. He clears a space and puts down the tray. He leans over her, speaking in a very faint voice.*)
   My heart will break clean open, girl. Nothing will ever be the same again, not nothing.
   (*She stirs slightly.*)
   Lucy—?

(*She is still again. He waits.*)
Perhaps—perhaps there *is* another shore where your Mam
is waiting—
(*Silence.*)
But I shan't bear it down here. I shan't bear it.
(*Silence.*)
Do you remember how I used to take you for a walk on the
Bluff. Lift you up on my shoulders. (*Choked*) Little flop of
blue ribbon in your hair. Nice clean white socks. Little legs
like—
(*Pause. He fights to control himself.*)
Like a little china doll.
(*She stirs. He swallows, fights back tears.*)
Lucy—?
LUCY: Dad?
(*They look at each other a tiny moment. A bit too late, he becomes
jaunty.*)
JOE: Sleep! Sleep! You're a Rip Van Winkle, my girl! I've
brought you up something nice.
LUCY: (*Dry mouthed*) I—sorry, Dad. I don't really want it at the
moment.
JOE: (*Hearty*) Oh it's only a bit, now! Nice bowl of tomato soup.
LUCY: A bit later, perhaps—
JOE: It's not out of a tin, mind. This is *real*, this is.
(*He spoons it up, and lets it fall back into the dish.*)
Lovely, it is, see!
LUCY: (*Smile*) I'll try. Only a bit, mind.
JOE: (*Pleased*) This is better than that stuff in the hospital. Put
some real good–ness in you, this will!
(*But she can't hold the tray, and she can't hold the spoon.*)
LUCY: Awkward. This tray . . .
JOE: (*Shocked*) Dear Jesus—you—
(*He sits on the bed.*)
I'll feed you, my love. I'll feed you. You've got to *eat*.
LUCY: Just one spoonful, then.
(*He puts the spoon to her mouth.*)
JOE: (*Coaxing*) Beautiful, this is—

LUCY: Yes. Thank you, Dad.
JOE: Some more? Drop more, eh?
(*She shakes her head.*)
Would you rather have something else?
(*She shakes her head.*)
The doctor will be here in a minute. Is it bad, girl? (*Thick voiced*) Is the pain bad, my lovely?
(*She shakes her head.*)

20. LUCY'S BEDROOM
LUCY *watching with patient interest as a young* DOCTOR *injects drug into her arm. He swabs it, finishing.*
LUCY: Thank you.
DOCTOR: (*Smile*) Thank *you*.
LUCY: What for?
DOCTOR: Courtesy, I suppose. I don't know.
LUCY: Courtesy. . . ?
(*He is putting stuff away in his bag. Puts cushion under her elbow.*)
DOCTOR: Let's call it that.
LUCY: They don't like you very much in this town, you know.
DOCTOR: Don't they?
(*She struggles a bit.*)
LUCY: Old Dr Hastings, he— (*Stops, gasps.*)
DOCTOR: (*Soft*) Steady.
LUCY: Old Dr Hastings took snuff, looked at the ceiling and told people to 'pull themselves together'.
DOCTOR: (*Slightly bitter laugh*) Yes. I know. Head over there. Heart over here. Soul somewhere in between. Pull themselves all together—hey presto, one fit human.
LUCY: He put more people in the churchyard than any other poisoner in history.
DOCTOR: Well—(*He sits down again.*)
LUCY: (*Deliberately, comically Welsh*) But they trusted him, see.
(*He laughs, but breaks off as a sudden wave of pain smacks into her.*)
DOCTOR: The drug will help. It'll help in a minute.
(*He looks on helpless as she struggles to regain mastery.*)

123

LUCY: (*Gasp*) What do—what do people—

DOCTOR: No, no. Don't talk.

LUCY: (*Determined*) What do they do at the—at the moment of death?

(*Pause.*)

DOCTOR: Lucy—I—

LUCY: (*Almost excited*) Just as they die, I mean—as they—at the very exact exact exact moment they—*cease.*

DOCTOR: Oh now, that—

(*She almost screams as the pain crunches her up. He grabs her arm.*)
A minute. Less. Less. It'll ease—

(*A struggle. She subsides.*)

LUCY: (*Pant*) Yes. I can feel it—yes—

DOCTOR: Easier?

(*She nods.*)

LUCY: I want to—*know.*

DOCTOR: I—Lucy. I don't think I can give you any one answer.

LUCY: (*Stronger*) Do they *acknowledge* it in any way? Do they?

DOCTOR: (*Uncomfortable*) You are—well— (*Little smile*) —sort of breaking the rules, Lucy.

LUCY: No point in keeping to any rules now. Is there?

(*Pause.*)

DOCTOR: No.

LUCY: You *must* have witnessed it. Often.

DOCTOR: Oh come on, I'm not *that* bad a doctor.

LUCY: I would like to know.

DOCTOR: Every doctor eventually expects his patient to *collude* with him, Lucy. Most *real* things are left unsaid. But that doesn't mean people don't understand.

LUCY: Only, I've seen animals die.

DOCTOR: Killed, you mean? But that's diff—

LUCY: No—die. I've seen it downstairs. Different animals, over the years, for different reasons—

DOCTOR: (*Nervous*) And?

LUCY: (*With awe*) They *know.* (*Swallow.*) They sort of hood their eyes and— (*pleased*) relax.

DOCTOR: Yes.

LUCY: (*Incantatory*) Relax. They relax, relax. And *let go*.
  (*The* DOCTOR *seems to come to a decision.*)
DOCTOR: That's it, Lucy. Yes. That's it exactly.
LUCY: (*Swift*) Don't lie to me.
DOCTOR: Lucy—listen—
LUCY: (*In a gust of panic*) Don't lie to me!
DOCTOR: (*Careful, steadily*) I'll say this, Lucy, and it is the truth.
  Almost any doctor will tell you the same thing. I have
  never known, repeat, never known, a person die who,
  knowing exactly what was happening at that exact
  moment, did not *accept* it in peace.
  (*She stares at him.*)
LUCY: And serenity?
  (*Slight pause.*)
DOCTOR: (*Repeats different word*) In peace.
LUCY: You mean—you mean—something natural—takes over.
  Like the animals.
DOCTOR: Yes. And that—
  (*He stops.*)
LUCY: Yes?
DOCTOR: (*Embarrassed*) It's beside the point really. But I
  think—yes, I think that's one of the very few reasons why I
  personally believe in—well, God.
  (*She looks at him.*)
  Sorry.
  (*A long pause.*)
LUCY: Help my father, won't you?
DOCTOR: Yes.
LUCY: I think he wants everything and everyone in the world to
  die—if—if I—
DOCTOR: Lucy—it is—natural. In part.
LUCY: Help my Dad.
  (*He nods his head quickly.*)
DOCTOR: Now go to sleep. You need it. I'll see you in the
  morning. You'll find that—
  (*He breaks off as the pain, too soon, crashes back. He holds on to
  her. Then quickly goes to his bag to get a new syringe. Swift,*

125

efficient, he gives her what will be the last injection.)
(*Whisper*) It'll go. It'll go. It'll go. It will go. Good girl.
Good girl.

21. CAR DRIVING SOUTH
The COMEDIAN, *with clenched hands on steering wheel, clenched face, eyes
staring hard ahead at the winding ribbon of road.*
  SALLY *looking at him, half furtively.*
  The speedometer needle still climbing.
SALLY: (*Trying to be moderate*) Too fast, Bobby.
  (*He does not answer. Zooming, zooming, zooming. She is looking at
  him.*)
  Bobby?
  (*His eyes flicker for the first time.*)
COMEDIAN: You know the one word you can never ever use in a
  joke—not anywhere?
SALLY: Please slow down.
  (*He hunches behind steering wheel like a racing driver.*)
COMEDIAN: Nigger you can say. Tit you can say. Even shit you
  can say. Virgin you can say. Pregnant you can say—
SALLY: Bobby!
COMEDIAN: Deaf you can say. Dumb you can say. Mad you can
  say. Piss you can say. Dwarf you can say. Fanny you can
  say. Blind. Cross-eyed, you can say— (*Sucks in breath.*) God
  you can say. All good jokes. All used up on the circuit.
  (*Zooming, zooming. She is looking at him, puzzled, tender and
  scared.*)
  But one word they won't have. They won't have—
  (*He turns and looks at her.*)
SALLY: Please—!
COMEDIAN: Cancer. Never ever use that word in a joke.
SALLY: Cancer.
COMEDIAN: (*His face all but crumpling*) Not her—please—God, not
  our Lucy . . .
SALLY: Perhaps she—well—it's not—I mean—
COMEDIAN: (*Snarl*) A matter of days. Or hours. So shut your
  stupid mouth!

126

SALLY: Yes.
> (*Pause.*)

COMEDIAN: Sally?

SALLY: (*Slightly sullen*) What?

COMEDIAN: Let's get married. Please.
> (*She is utterly astonished, and turns her face away, wanting to cry with shock.*)
>
> I know . . . I know . . .

SALLY: (*Thick*) Bobby?
> (*Pause. Zooming landscape.*)

COMEDIAN: She—she used to sit in the shop, 7 or 8 years old, talking to those bloody animals. She cried when the blue-tongued skink was sold to this old collier. A bloody great lizard, I ask you. We can make a go of it, Sally. Surely, we/ can?

SALLY: If—if you mean it. Really mean it. . . ?

COMEDIAN: Oh, yes. I mean it. I mean it.
> (*Close-up* SALLY, *extremely puzzled, but moved.*)

22. PET SHOP

The cockatoo is cocking its head. A portrait. Then it shrieks.

JOE: Shut up! Shut up, the doctor will be here any minute, you great fool!
> (*Man and bird again seem to examine each other intently.*)
>
> (*Soft*) All right. All right. It's all right. Pretty birdie. Pretty, pretty bird.
>
> (*Shop door opens.*)

CUSTOMER: Good morning, Joe.
> (JOE *still gazing at bird, accepting something inside himself.*)
>
> Looks like a bit more wet, then.

JOE: (*Turning*) What? Oh. Morning, Owen.

CUSTOMER: Rain. Again. By the looks of it.
> (*The* CUSTOMER *has a cold.*)

JOE: Rain. Yes.

CUSTOMER: As though we haven't had enough, eh?
> (JOE *glances at the stair.*)

JOE: What can I do for you, Owen?

127

Joe's Ark

CUSTOMER: (*Sniff.*) A dog collar. Oh, this cold!

JOE: Collar?

CUSTOMER: Nice posh one. With studs on. A real nice one, Joe. Got one to suit?

JOE: Plenty of collars, mun.

CUSTOMER: Our Huw wants to give Micky a new collar for his birthday. Soft, ennit!

JOE: (*Abstracted*) Lot of collars—studs—yes . . .

CUSTOMER: Bloody dog. More trouble than it's worth. But got to keep the kids happy, see. How's Lucy?

(*The* DOCTOR *comes in.*)

DOCTOR: Morning, Mr Jones.

JOE: Morning.

CUSTOMER: Mornin', Doctor.

JOE: Studs. Spikey like, you mean?

(*His mind is with the* DOCTOR, *who goes through and up the stairs.*)

CUSTOMER: Poking out a bit. That dog's got no belly at all—he'll run away from a spider. The sort of collar that real savage dogs have. You know. (*Sniff.*) Any better is she? Your girl?

JOE: (*Irritated*) Can't say. Can't say.

(JOE *looks anxiously towards stair.*)

CUSTOMER: Only our Glad told me to ask, like. Yes—one like that. Good strong collar. (*Inquisitive*) Is your Bob coming home, Joe?

JOE: (*Curt*) That's family, ennit?

CUSTOMER: Sorry. Hope you don't think I'm poking my nose in, only our Glad thought as—yes. That one will do nice, Joe.

(*A middle-aged* WOMAN CUSTOMER *enters.*)

JOE: Good collar, this is. Very well made.

CUSTOMER: I seen that young man you got staying with you, in the breadshop. Useful. Friend of Lucy, would that be?

JOE: (*Hostile*) Is there anything else?

CUSTOMER: No. No, that'll do nicely—

(*But* JOE's *attention is caught by the* DOCTOR. *The* DOCTOR, *looking a bit agitated, beckons urgently to* JOE *from the foot of the stairs at back of shop.* JOE *hurtles across without a word.* MAN *and*

128

WOMAN CUSTOMERS *look at each other*).

Well now. Well, well . . .

(JOE *and* DOCTOR *in brief but earnest conversation at foot of the stair.* JOE *goes up stair, face contorting.* DOCTOR *hesitates at foot of stair.*)

WOMAN: What's up then? Is it—?

CUSTOMER: (*Sniff.*) Lucy. I expect.

WOMAN: Ah, poor little thing!

(*They both look at the* DOCTOR, *hovering strangely at bottom of stair.* CUSTOMER *holds back a sneeze.*)

CUSTOMER: Mind, I'm feeling pretty rough myself.

(DOCTOR *comes on through shop.*)

CUSTOMER *and* WOMAN: Good morning, Doctor.

DOCTOR: Oh. Ah. Good morning . . .

CUSTOMER: Excuse me, Doctor—?

(*He breaks stride.*)

DOCTOR: Yes?

CUSTOMER: (*Fawning*) Didn't like to bother you at the surgery this morning, see—but I've got this dreadful cold and—

DOCTOR: (*Astounded*) What?

CUSTOMER: Well, if I could have a paper for being off work, it'd save me—

DOCTOR: (*Furious*) You know the surgery hours. You're wasting my time. Dammit no. No!

(*And he stalks out, white and shaken. Pause.*)

CUSTOMER: (*To* WOMAN) That's never *right*, is it? That's a disgrace, that is!

WOMAN: He's not a bit like poor old Dr Hastings. Rude, that was.

CUSTOMER: Not in the same class! He's not worth tuppence! A cold like mine—well!

23. LUCY'S BEDROOM

JOE *is seen, as though from the bed, backing slowly away from the bed, his face astonished, unbelieving. He stops. He comes forward again. Now we see the bed. He takes hold of* LUCY's *hand. Now we see* LUCY's *face, placid, dead.*

129

JOE: (*Whisper, almost inaudible*) Paid â gadael iddi farw, ni allwn
ddal y boen. Cymer fi a'r hyn oll sydd gennyf yn ei lle, ie,
cymer fi, a gad i'r eneth fach gael byw.*
(*Silence. From below, like an answer, the muted sound of the
cockatoo's cry.* JOE *turns away, grief breaking.*)

24. PET SHOP
The COMEDIAN *comes in, and looks at the cockatoo.*
COMEDIAN: (*Wry*) Christ—hasn't he sold you *yet!*
(JOHN *comes into shop, trying to hold open door for* SALLY *and keep
control of grocery bags. The* COMEDIAN *looks at the stair. His face
changes.*)

25. STAIRCASE
Past the turn in the stair, shop contents now out of sight, JOE *and his son
come face to face.*
They look at each other for a moment. There is no room to pass.
COMEDIAN: (*Dry mouthed*) How—how—Dad—? How is she—?
(*Fractional pause.*)
JOE: She's with your Mam.
(*Fractional pause of shock. Then the* COMEDIAN *covers his face with
both hands.* JOE *looks at him steadily, almost coldly.*)
A minute ago, Bob. Just one minute. I was with her.
COMEDIAN: (*Crying*) Did she—was she— Oh Dad—?
JOE: (*Holding himself in*) She said—she said she was—going
home. She sent her love and said she was going home.
(*Pause. As though to a child*) That's where your Mam is, see.
(*Then in a sudden mutual impulse the two men hold on to each other,
in a sort of desperation and yet also a comfort. But they pull apart
quickly, shocked.*)
COMEDIAN: (*Angry*) I should have heard sooner. And you should
have written yourself!
JOE: (*Severely*) Let me go by, Robert. Let me pass.

---

*Please, please do not let it happen. Please. Take me instead, and all my
animals. Take me and let her live!

COMEDIAN: There's your *prayers* for you! There's your prayers
—see?
(*Silence.*)

JOE: Yes, I know.

COMEDIAN: (*Ashamed*) No. No, Dad. No, no—
(*He puts his hand on* JOE's *arm.* JOE *shakes it off.*)

JOE: And there's your *jokes* for you! There's your dirty jokes—*see?*

COMEDIAN: No, Dad. Please, Dad. No, no Dad . . .
(*Pause.*)

JOE: Let's go up and see her, boy. Let's go and—and—lovely she
is now. Come you on, our Bobby.
(*He turns to go back up, then as though struck by a new thought,
looks over shoulder.*)
Is it raining out?

COMEDIAN: What? No—no. I don't think so. *Why?*

JOE: (*Going on up*) I just wanted to know. I didn't want the rain,
see. I didn't want it to be raining. Not for our Lucy—
(*The* COMEDIAN *follows him on up, shaking his head. The cockatoo
sounds again, a cry on the empty stair.*)

26. THE PET SHOP
The big bird, cocking its head, alert, beautiful. It calls, eyes glittering.

131

Cream in My Coffee

Cream in My Coffee was produced by London Weekend Television in association with PFH Ltd and first transmitted by the ITV Network on 2 November 1980. The cast was as follows:

BERNARD WILSHER	Lionel Jeffries
YOUNG BERNARD	Peter Chelsom
JEAN WILSHER	Peggy Ashcroft
YOUNG JEAN	Shelagh McLeod
JACK BUTCHER	Martin Shaw
MRS WILSHER	Faith Brook
HOTEL PORTER (1979)	Leo Dollan
HOTEL PORTER (1938)	Will Stampe
GIRL IN POOL	Tracy Eddon
MAID	Dawn Perliman
WAITRESS	Pik-Sen Lim
TOUT	Walter Sparrow
WAITER	Howard Attfield
VICAR	Robert Fyfe

Executive Producer	Tony Wharmby
Producer	Kenith Trodd
Director	Gavin Millar
Designer	John Emery

On the Sunday evenings of long ago I used to sit in a tin bath in the kitchen lathering myself with a large block of rancid green soap while the wireless on the other side of the dark brown curtain would be slowly exhausting its accumulator with four minutes of Waldteufel twinklingly suspended between the Roses of Picardy and a moonlit interlude set In a Monastery Garden. I used to make an audible groan whenever the incredibly plummy announcer said that we were now going 'over to the Palm Court of the Grand Hotel', and the soapy water no doubt splashed out upon the linoleum. In truth, though, the music was always more seductive —'charming' is the word I have not been searching for—than I was ever prepared to allow. The programme was broadcast with a quite distinct, peculiarly ceramic sort of resonance, dangerously close to an echo, and when I think of it now I seem to conjure up not green soap and brown curtain but the act of delicately breaking off a piece of Madeira cake on a plain, brilliantly white tea plate.

The hotel in question was the Grand Hotel, Eastbourne, a huge creamy palace which looks out to the sea across a stone dolphin and triangular beds of excessively neat flowers. It must have worked its way into my mind, along with the Skater's Waltz and 'In a Persian Market Place', first as something inaccessibly exotic and then, after many years, as something impossibly quaint. My media-numbed acquaintances expressed an almost scornful amusement, and my family a forehead-puckering consternation, when I decided to have a week's holiday in the very selfsame place in the summer of 1979. I always find it difficult to explain that I keep my vengeance for places and things, not people, so that if ever I do buy a Rolls-Royce it will be precisely in order to neglect and eventually humiliate it.

In the event, the holiday was just about the best one I have

135

ever had, even allowing for the fact that I love things English and do my level best to behave as though I were a not altogether amiable eccentric. The trouble was, I did not know at the time that I was enjoying myself, being too busily occupied in finding fault with everything in sight, and everything not there, with such a hungry diligence that I even complained about the click–click of the wooden toggles against the window frames.

I was looking for the past, of course, and would more readily have accepted the cream cakes at tea time if they had been drenched in formaldehyde. Early evening drinks in a splendidly vaulted salon were curdled for me by a piano afflicted with the succubus of an electronic attachment. Well aware by now that the soapy ghost of lost Sunday evenings could not be assuaged, I fell to thinking (and the language duplicates the perversity of my then mood) about how some peppery old sod of the kind I eventually hope to become would feel if he ever returned to such subverted munificence.

The shell of an idea for a play can be absurd and trivial, and its first emotions a mere second-order indulgence. Such was the case with this one, and I must have sat down to begin writing it with a sneer on my face and the saving intention of destroying every last vestige of it by the time I had inscribed an encephalitic 9 at the top of the appropriate page. I have lost count of the number of times this has happened, but bless each occasion not so much for my reputation as my self-respect.

The actual labour of writing, however, can mercifully refuse to collude with the banalities of the original design. I *did* destroy my first half-dozen or so pages, but only to go back to the beginning again. And again. The slow and then the swifter swing between the past and the present became more than the simple difference between things as they were or might have been and things as they are or seem to be. The shape of a life, of two lives, began to ride the swing. The gaps separating ardour from resignation, promise from betrayal, innocence from knowledge, yawned more and more open, and then kept closing again.

There are passages in this play, and moments in the other two in this volume, which escape to tell me that buried somewhere in myself is a better and more wholesome writer than I have yet found out how to be. I do not know how to coax him out into the open, and the stubborn recluse may never agree to emerge at all. But it is the thought of his presence, however illusory, which makes holding a pen the most challenging, the most exhilarating, thing I could ever do.

One great danger: talking about it. Better four minutes with Waldteufel and a stroll through the Monastery Garden, freshly clean with green soap, on the far side of something far more difficult than a brown curtain to pull aside.

Cream in My Coffee

1. A GRAND SOUTH COAST HOTEL
A huge, white, wedding-cake of a five-star hotel, crenellated and towered, against a blue sky. We move in slowly from the sea, across the shingled beach decorated with luscious brown bodies, looking at the grand Victorian palace as though licking it, lovingly, like a huge ice-cream.

On the move, the voice of Sam Browne (with the Jack Hylton Orchestra) singing the 1930s' hit 'You're the Cream in My Coffee'.
SINGER: You're the cream in my coffee
You're the salt in my stew
You will always be
My necessity
I'd be lost without you.

You're the starch in my collar
You're the lace in my shoe
You will always be
My necessity
I'd be lost without you.
(*On the last two lines we go . . .*)

2. INSIDE THE HOTEL: 1979
An old PORTER, *in hotel livery, is trundling heavily and seemingly not too willingly along a wide hotel corridor leading endlessly away from the lifts. He is carrying two fat and obviously expensive suitcases.*

Behind him, looking around them, come a man and a woman. She is in her early sixties, he is in his late sixties. They are BERNARD *and* JEAN WILSHER—*and as though by now unused to it, by a self-consciously deliberate act, they are holding hands.*
BERNARD: It's a long way from the lift.
PORTER: No, it ain't. 'S only four and a half miles, sir.
(JEAN *laughs.* BERNARD, *however, is not so sure that the answer isn't a little impertinent.*)

139

JEAN: (*Nervous little laugh*) Still, we came for the exercise.

PORTER: What room is it?

BERNARD: (*Severely*) You've got the keys.

(JEAN *looks at her husband. She is a much warmer person. There is something tight and tensed up about him.*)

JEAN: It's 343, actually.

PORTER: Oh, yes. A suite. It's a very nice room that one. One of the best in the place.

BERNARD: (*To please his wife*) Glad to hear it.

PORTER: Looks right across to the sea, and right down on the swimming pool. You can near enough dive in. If you don't mind breaking your neck.

(*Through the open windows, the sound of gulls.* JEAN *tilts her head back happily.*)

JEAN: (*To* BERNARD) Listen, dear. Isn't that one of *the* most evocative sounds. *Desert Island Discs.*

PORTER: Drives you barmy in the end.

BERNARD: (*Sharply*) Evidently so.

(*The* PORTER *at last senses that* BERNARD *is one of the 'awkward ones'.*)

PORTER: Here we are, sir: 343.

(*He opens door—into the past.*)

3. SUITE 343: 1938

Door opens for two attractive young people: JEAN, *aged about 20, and her brand new husband-to-be* BERNARD WILSHER, *aged about 26.*

JEAN: (*Enthusiastically*) Oh, a lovely little hallway. All our own!

(BERNARD *grins at her very shyly. He has the appearance of a would-be young buck who can't quite pull it off.*)

PORTER: (*Grandly*) And this, Madam, is the Sitting Room.

BERNARD: (*Nervous smile*) Very nice, isn't it?

(JEAN *gives him a supposedly 'wicked' sidelong glance.*)

JEAN: Oh, yes! *My* husband will like this room. Exactly what we required, isn't it, darling?

(BERNARD *gives an embarrassed and give-away little cough.*)

BERNARD: Yes. Oh. Quite. Absolutely.

Cream in My Coffee

(The PORTER *looks at him with a knowing smile. They always know.)*

PORTER: And there's a Very Nice Little Bedroom through here, sir . . .

(He goes to show them.)

BERNARD: *(Quickly)* Yes. No need to—ah—we'll manage now, thank you very much . . . just um . . . *(Awkwardly he tips the* PORTER, *who quickly examines the coin, then responds ingratiatingly.)*

PORTER: Very nice of you, sir. Very nice indeed. I hope you and madam will have a very nice stay here.

JEAN *and* BERNARD: Thank you.

(The PORTER *all but bows and scrapes out of the door. The outer door shuts. They look at each other a moment, pleased and furtive and giggly.)*

JEAN: Crikey! Half-a-crown, wasn't it!

BERNARD: I *know.* I'm not very good at this. I was all fingers and thumbs when he mentioned The Bedroom.

(He rolls his eyes in mock lasciviousness at her: a merry fellow. She laughs and goes into his arms.)

JEAN: Oh, Bernard. Do you think they know?

(He kisses her.)

BERNARD: Who cares?

JEAN: *I* care. *(He kisses again.)* I don't want them to think of me as one of *those* ladies. *(She responds.)* Mmmm. Oh, darling. Darling . . .

BERNARD: *(Kissing again)* But that's just what you are. A loose woman!

(She steps back a bit, a little unsure.)

JEAN: Bernard?

(He laughs, tenderly, and pulls her back into him.)

BERNARD: Of course you're not, Jean! Don't be such a goose!

JEAN: It *is* a bit naughty, though.

(She giggles again, half wanting to be thought 'fast'.)

BERNARD: No, it isn't. It really isn't. We *are* going to be man-and-wife after all.

(But he cannot quite avoid a tinge of anxiety.)

141

Cream in My Coffee

JEAN: Roll on September.
BERNARD: Roll on tonight!
(She laughs nervously. They kiss yet again. She pulls back.)
JEAN: *(Wickedly)* Bernard—is that a pipe in your trouser
   pocket—?
BERNARD: *(Embarrassed)* Oh, I say—!
*(They look at each other a moment, then burst out laughing. But in a
way that shows how relatively unsure of each other they still are.)*

4. SUITE 343: 1979
Forty-one years on, BERNARD, *in one of the armchairs, tamps down
tobacco preparatory to lighting his pipe.*
JEAN: You're surely not going to light up *now* are you Bernard?
BERNARD: *(Irritated)* What?
JEAN: Think of what the doctor said—can't you?
BERNARD: If I did everything they say, I might as well pack it in
   anyway.
JEAN: I suppose I'd better unpack.
BERNARD: There's no hurry. Why are you always in such a
   hurry?
JEAN: We don't want our clothes to be creased, do we?
*(His whole posture, his whole expression, shows that he has gone far
beyond mere irritability into something approaching dangerous
hypertension.)*
BERNARD: Why are you so damned argumentative, Jean? It gets
   on my nerves.
JEAN: Argumentative? Me?
BERNARD: About the blasted clothes.
JEAN: All I said was that we don't want our clothes to be
   creased.
BERNARD: No, you didn't. You said, 'We don't want our clothes
   to be creased, *do we?*' It's that bloody, never ending 'do we?'
   The way you seem to make a perfectly ordinary, perfectly
   reasonable statement sound combative and—
*(He stops, hearing the grating excess in his own tongue, feeling the
tense irritability in his own limbs. She looks at him, sad.)*
JEAN: I feel half afraid to say anything at all nowadays.

(*He makes a gesture, half apology and yet half an obscure inner rage.*)

BERNARD: I don't know what's wrong. I don't know why I— Look, Jean. Let's hope these few days work, eh? Sorry, old girl.

JEAN: I think this is the same room. The very same.

BERNARD: Is it? (*Sigh.*) Doesn't look half so grand somehow. A bit stale, don't you think?

JEAN: We've grown used to better things. We thought it was marvellous. I'd never been in such a spiffing place.

BERNARD: Whenever you go back anywhere, it's like looking through the wrong end of the telescope. Perhaps it wasn't such a good idea to come here again.

JEAN: Oh, I don't know. You can't go abroad, the way you are. We're only an hour or so away from home.

BERNARD: From the hospital you mean.

JEAN: No, from *home*, Bernard.

(*At last, he lights the pipe he has been clenching.*)

BERNARD: (*Between puffs*) Food should be all right. It's still a five-star rating here. (*Gloomily*) Sea air might give us an appetite.

(*She has wandered over to one of the windows, and is looking out rather wistfully.*)

JEAN: The pool is still there.

BERNARD: What?

JEAN: The swimming pool. With a stone dolphin. It's still there.

BERNARD: Well, I shan't be going in. That's for sure.

JEAN: No.

BERNARD: Too many old people make fools of themselves.

JEAN: We can sit by the side, though. In the sun. Can't we?

BERNARD: (*Gratingly*) Why is it that almost everything you say nowadays is in the form of a question?

JEAN: What do you mean?

BERNARD: There! You see!

(*She turns her face back to the window. Her eyes are glazing with unshed tears. She can see—*)

Cream in My Coffee

5. HOTEL SWIMMING POOL: 1979

Where, in some boisterous play, THREE YOUNG MEN *in swimming trunks are carrying a laughing, protesting, struggling* YOUNG WOMAN *in light summer clothing to the edge of the pool.*

GIRL: (*Half scream, half laugh*) No! I can't swim! I can't—
No–o–ooo!
(*But, laughing and shouting, they throw her in. Her long black hair floats out behind her on the water and then, as the* MEN *laugh, she slowly sinks, without any trace of struggle. The laughter suddenly stops.*)

MAN: (*Startled shout*) Carol!

6. SUITE 343: 1979

Shock and horror on JEAN's *face, as she looks down on the scene.*

JEAN: Oh my God! Bernard—!

7. THE SWIMMING POOL: 1979

TWO *of the* MEN, *with quicker reactions than the* THIRD, *dive in and thrash across to the apparently drowning* CAROL.

As they reach her, she eludes their clutching grasp, crashes their heads together, surfaces, and swims with ease and grace out of their reach.

The THIRD MAN *jumps up and down with amused delight.*

8. SUITE 343: 1979

JEAN's *hands have fluttered up to her face. They are coming down now, with relief and a sort of amusement.*

JEAN: Oh! Naughty girl!
(BERNARD *has not stirred.*)

BERNARD: What's going on?
(*She turns, amusement on her face—she is naturally an eager talker, a warm 'gossip'—but—*)

JEAN: Those young men down there threw this girl into the pool and she pretended she couldn't—
(*Her voice trails off, something about his face, his manner, takes the words from her.*)

BERNARD: Pretended she couldn't what?

JEAN: Never mind.

Cream in My Coffee

(He doesn't notice the hurt.)
BERNARD: Shall we have some tea?
JEAN: If you like.
BERNARD: What's the matter?
JEAN: Nothing.
BERNARD: Well—*do* you want tea, or *don't* you?
JEAN: Yes. If you like.
BERNARD: Haven't you got a mind of your own?
JEAN: No, Bernard. I don't think I have.

9. THE HOTEL LOUNGE: 1938
Huge colonnaded lounge in the old 'grand' manner. The scattered, ample armchairs and tables are nearly all occupied. WAITRESSES or MAIDS in little caps and frilly aprons, etc., are serving silver trays of tea and buttered scones and cream cakes and macaroons, etc. A tea-time STRING TRIO, on an oval platform, is scraping sweetly through 'The Isle of Capri'.
> BERNARD *and* JEAN *(the young couple) are seated by a long window awaiting their afternoon tea.* JEAN*'s eyes are sparkling with delight.* BERNARD *is rather covertly looking at her, enraptured more by her than anything around them.*
BERNARD: You look like a little girl at her first grown-up party.
JEAN: *Do* I, Bernard?
BERNARD: Have you got little lights in your eyes, or what?
JEAN: *(Coy)* What do you mean?
> *(But he stiffens into a wary silence as a frilly* WAITRESS *brings their tea and cakes.)*
MAID: Tea for two.
BERNARD: Yes. Thank you.
JEAN: Oh, what lovely big macaroons. *My husband* loves macaroons.
MAID: They are nice, madam.
> *(*BERNARD *coughs nervously.)*
BERNARD: Yes. They are.
MAID: Will that be all, then, sir?
JEAN: Crumbs, yes. We shall get as fat as mud. But—there's a

bigger band in the evenings, isn't there?
MAID: A proper band, yes, madam.
JEAN: I should hope so, too. My husband and I like to—
BERNARD: (*Quickly*) Of course there is, dear.
(*The* WAITRESS *smiles and withdraws.*)
JEAN: Shall I be mother?
(*She reaches for the teapot, with a pretty little giggle.*)
BERNARD: (*Hesitantly*) Jean—I wish you wouldn't keep—um—I
mean, isn't it a bit silly the way you draw attention to the
fact that we're not—um—married—?
JEAN: (*Wide-eyed*) Do I?
BERNARD: Well—yes. You do rather. Every time you say 'my
husband' this or 'my husband' that . . .
JEAN: Don't you like me saying that, Bernard?
BERNARD: Of course I do, darling. But—
(*She is very hurt, however.*)
JEAN: You think I'm *gauche*, don't you?
(*Alarmed, he reaches for her hand—*)
BERNARD: Don't be silly, angel—
(*But she pulls her hand away, ready to be tearful.*)
JEAN: Oh yes you do! You think I'm—*immature.*
BERNARD: Jean, darling. I never said anything of the sort.
JEAN: Yes you did, too! You said I was like a little girl at a
grown-ups' party—
BERNARD: I meant that you were so pretty and—
JEAN: (*Rising tone*) Immature! That's obviously what you meant.
(*Voice breaks.*) You're ashamed of me. I can see you are.
(*He looks anxiously around.*)
BERNARD: Jean—don't, my love— People are looking—
JEAN: That's half the trouble, Bernard. You care more about
what other people are thinking than you do of *me.*
(*Her eyes are filling, her voice is boo-hoo, and he becomes aware that,
yes, people are now casting a curious glance or two—*)
BERNARD: Control yourself, darling. Please.
(*But she is stoking herself up.*)
JEAN: If it's going to be you correcting me all the time when we're
married, perhaps we ought to think the whole thing over . . .

BERNARD: Oh, lovey-dove. Please don't. Not here. Why
   don't you stop being so silly and pour the tea, mmm?

JEAN: Don't you talk to me like that. You're not my father. You
   don't own me—not yet you don't!
   (*He smiles awkwardly at a watching face, then, almost out of the
   side of his mouth—*)

BERNARD: All right. All right. I'll pour the bloody tea!

JEAN: (*Aghast*) You swore at me! You *swore*, Bernard.
   (*Not only aghast but rather loud.*)

BERNARD: (*Mutter*) For Christ's sake, Jean. What's the matter
   with you?

JEAN: I didn't know you were like this. (*Half sob*) I had no idea
   you were such a bully.
   (*She is upset, but, even more so, she is secretly enjoying herself. The
   TRIO has moved into 'Red Sails in the Sunset'.*)

BERNARD: (*Goaded*) And I had no idea you were such a ninny!
   (*Her mouth falls open.*)

JEAN: Ohhh!

BERNARD: (*Alarmed*) I didn't mean it—
   (*But, hand to her mouth, and excessively melodramatic, she rushes
   from the table. He rises, calls her name, then realizes that people are
   looking, and, extremely flustered, sits down again. Awkwardly alone,
   he takes a cream cake, stiffly trying to maintain his dignity, and
   bites into it. The cream squirts out, messily, down the lapel of his
   jacket.*)

10. THE LOBBY: 1938
*Genuinely upset now, and feeling ridiculous, JEAN scurries out of the huge
lounge into the broad, chandeliered reception hall, head down, hand to her
mouth.*

   *Reaching the lifts, she all but collides with a smooth man on the brink
of middle age with slick, brushed back, black hair. He is JACK BUTCHER,
a singer.*

BUTCHER: Oops-a-daisy.

JEAN: (*Upset*) I'm sorry—so sorry—

BUTCHER: Hey now. What's the matter, little lady?

JEAN: Nothing. It's—nothing.

147

BUTCHER: Is the big bad wolf after you?
> (*She looks at him.*)

JEAN: I'm—no— Excuse me, but— (*Her face glows*) —aren't you—?

BUTCHER: (*Smirk*) Jack Butcher. You've got me, little lady. The one and only. That's me.

JEAN: Oh. I—gosh! I've always liked the way you sing, Mr Butcher.
> (*He gives a little bow. An 'absolute charlatan', long since stranded in his own unhappy mid-Atlantic speech, through which cockney sometimes peeps.*)

BUTCHER: And I've always liked the way *you* look, Miss—ah—

JEAN: But you've never—

BUTCHER: Ah, but I have. In my dreams, I have.
> (*She looks at him in astonishment, then bursts out laughing. Behind her the lift doors open.*)

11. THE LIFTS: 1979

Elderly BERNARD *and* JEAN *come out of the lift.*

BERNARD: It's gone to the dogs. The place has gone to the dogs.
> (*She doesn't answer. They walk slowly into—*)

12. THE LOUNGE: 1979

Nowadays just a scatter of largely elderly couples scattered sparsely around the huge interconnecting rooms.

> BERNARD *and* JEAN *hesitate in dismay.*

JEAN: Oh, dear. Where is everyone?

BERNARD: Looks more like a geriatric ward.

JEAN: There *were* some young people at the pool.

BERNARD: Where shall we sit?

JEAN: Over by the windows.

BERNARD: I hope the cakes aren't as old as the clientele.
> (JEAN *laughs.*)

JEAN: Feeling better, are you, Bernard?
> (*He sinks into armchair.*)

BERNARD: I shall never feel much better. But—oof— (*As he settles —sometimes I *do* feel like a quiet chuckle. (*Looks at her with* *a sad smile.*) Nothing excessive, mind.

JEAN: (*Smile*) Nothing I'd notice, do you mean?

(*He grabs quickly and urgently at her hand.*)

BERNARD: I'm sorry, Jean. I'm very, very sorry.

JEAN: Now, now, Bernie.

BERNARD: I've been an absolute shit, I know. But—

(*He sucks in his breath and shakes his head.*)

JEAN: (*Smile*) A bear with a sore head.

(*At a near table, an* OLD MAN *has a bad fit of coughing. It wheezes and rattles and gurgles rather nastily.*)

BERNARD: (*With disgust*) Bloody hell!

JEAN: Not very nice, is it?

(*The* OLD MAN *at the near table wipes his mouth with a big spotted handkerchief.*)

BERNARD: (*Snarl*) Not very nice? It's totally disgust—

(*But suddenly he starts to laugh.*)

JEAN: Perhaps he swallowed the wrong way.

(BERNARD *looks at her, stops laughing, then in a sudden, strange surge starts to cough and laugh and fart at the same time, absolutely helplessly.*)

BERNARD: Wrong—way—?

JEAN: Bernard? (*As he farts*) Oh, Bernard, shhhh!

(*But he cannot stop. His laughter becomes totally helpless, virtually hysterical. A young hotel* WAITRESS *comes across, smiling uncertainly.*)

WAITRESS: Is everything all right?

JEAN: (*Sharply*) Bernard!

(*The uncertain smile dies on the* WAITRESS*'s face.* BERNARD*'s 'laughter' is now more obviously closer to pain than anything else.*)

WAITRESS: Hadn't we better—um—

JEAN: (*Scared*) Yes. Call a doctor. Quickly!

(*But in a great heave of self-control,* BERNARD *manages to stop laughing—just.*)

BERNARD: (*Gasp*) No—no—I'm— No, don't do that—

JEAN: Are you—are you sure, dear?

(BERNARD *nods, wipes tears from his eyes, blows his nose.*)

WAITRESS: (*Relieved*) Perhaps a nice hot pot of tea—?

149

JEAN: Yes. Oh yes, please.
> (*With a look half of anxiety and half of disgust, the lone* WAITRESS *goes away.* BERNARD *starts to laugh again.*)

BERNARD: The things— (*Gasp*) —the things—

JEAN: (*Desperate*) Oh, Bernard. Don't! Please don't!
> (*He brings himself back into control, with pain.*)

BERNARD: The things we have to . . . things we have to do to get service in this place.

JEAN: Yes, dear.
> (*He looks at the people looking at him.*)

BERNARD: (*Shout*) What are you all staring at?

JEAN: (*Quietly*) Don't, Bernard. It doesn't matter . . .
> (*The other* OLD MAN *at a table nearby starts to cough badly again.* BERNARD *glares across at him with a look of venomous hatred.* BERNARD's *cheek muscles start to twitch. Badly shaken, he puts his hand to his cheek, as though brushing something away.*)

BERNARD: Where's the tea, then? Where's the bloody tea?

JEAN: It's coming.

BERNARD: Is it? Is it coming? Where? I don't see it. I don't see it!

JEAN: You're making me so unhappy, Bernard. Try to—please, will you—?

BERNARD: Leave me alone!

JEAN: But *Bernard*—

BERNARD: Nag, nag, nag.
> (*Silence. Then he looks savagely around, drumming his fingers on the table, heavily.*)

JEAN: Have you got a pain, Bernard? Do you want to go back to the room—?
> (*His fingers stop drumming a moment, then—*)

BERNARD: There aren't any gnats in here, are there?
> (*Fractional pause.*)

JEAN: No.

BERNARD: Then they are at the back of my eyeballs. Floating around. Blobs. Small blobs. (*He smiles at her.*) They used to have a little string band in here at teatime, didn't they? Or was that somewhere else?

JEAN: No, it was here.

BERNARD: Wonder if any of them are still alive.

JEAN: Shouldn't think so. They were older. A lot older. Especially the violin player.

BERNARD: I don't remember.

JEAN: I can see her now. As if it was yesterday.

BERNARD: That's the trouble.

JEAN: What—?

BERNARD: Everything is as if it was yesterday. (*Looks at her, almost accusingly.*) Did I make a spectacle of myself?

JEAN: Well—no. But—

BERNARD: Did I?

JEAN: It doesn't really matter, does it?

BERNARD: Christ, how humiliating!

JEAN: It doesn't matter.

BERNARD: There was an old woman near where we lived when I was a boy— (*Then, with wonder*) Isn't it funny? Why should I think of her?

JEAN: (*With relief*) Ah. I think this must be our tea coming. (*They watch the* WAITRESS *approaching.*)

BERNARD: (*Suddenly*) She had a moustache. (*The* WAITRESS *darts a swift, wary glance at* BERNARD *as she puts the tray down.*)

WAITRESS: Here we are, then.

BERNARD: This isn't a geriatric ward, you know.

WAITRESS: Sorry?

JEAN: (*Quickly*) Thank you. That's lovely.

BERNARD: (*Mimic*) 'Here we are, then.' Tea for the old folks.

WAITRESS: (*Coldly*) I hope you enjoy it.

JEAN: Very kind of you. Thank you so much. (WAITRESS *goes away. Pause.*)

BERNARD: Well, I mean to say . . .

JEAN: You are making my life a misery, Bernard.

BERNARD: Shut up.

JEAN: Don't spoil it. Don't spoil everything. (*Pause. He works his mouth.*)

BERNARD: Ghastly cakes.

JEAN: They'll do. Shall I pour the tea?

151

Cream in My Coffee

(*And she does. He watches, then seems to drift away.*)

BERNARD: She had a moustache.

JEAN: Do you want a doughnut, or would you rather have an éclair?

(*He doesn't answer, so she puts a doughnut on his plate.*)

BERNARD: Lived in the most Godawful tumbledown wreck of a little cottage. All on her own. With a bit of sacking stuffed into one of the downstairs windows. Terrible. Garden just a mess of weed and couch grass— Yes. A doughnut will do very nicely. Thank you.

(*Pause. They eat.*)

(*Suddenly*) Puss! Puss!

JEAN: (*Startled*) What?

BERNARD: Old Mrs Teague. Yes. That was her name. She had this old tom-cat.

JEAN: What about her?

BERNARD: She had a moustache.

JEAN: You said that.

BERNARD: (*Venomously*) So have you.

JEAN: You're not going to spoil my holiday, Bernard. I'm not going to let you upset me, so there!

BERNARD: Poor old sod.

JEAN: (*Near tears*) I'm not going to take any notice. I'm *not*.

BERNARD: What?

JEAN: You can call me as many names as you like.

BERNARD: No, no. Old Mrs Teague. I'm talking about old Mrs Teague.

JEAN: Oh.

BERNARD: That's what's wrong with us, Jean. You never listen to me.

JEAN: I'm sorry.

BERNARD: You're not interested in the things I have to say. I don't know whether you are there or not half the time.

JEAN: Drink your tea. Don't let it get cold. There's nothing worse than cold tea.

(*He does as he is told, then, as though realizing it, rattles the cup back down on to the saucer, angrily. She takes no notice. Silence.*)

BERNARD: (*Eventually*) I don't suppose she was a day older than I am now.

(*As we look at his old, suddenly almost wistful face, we hear—*)

SINGER: (*Off*) I'm not a poet
   How well I know it
   I've never been a raver
   But when I speak of you
   I rave a bit, it's true
   I'm wild about you
   I'm lost without you
   You give my life its flavour
   What sugar does for tea
   That's what you do for me—
(*During which, from his puzzled, troubled, rheumily ruminative face, the past slowly forms into—*)

13. HOTEL BALLROOM: 1938

JACK BUTCHER *is at the microphone, in front of the dance band, singing (that is, miming to the voice of the original 1930s' recording).*

BUTCHER: (*Sings*) You're the cream in my coffee
   You're the salt in my stew
   You will always be
   My necessity
   I'd be lost without you

   You're the starch in my collar
   You're the lace in my shoe
   You will always be
   My necessity
   I'd be lost without you.
(*And, in a dressy atmosphere, we pick out young* JEAN *and* BERNARD *on the huge ballroom floor among other elegant dancers. They have eyes for each other only.*)
   Most men tell love tales
   And each phrase dovetails
   You've heard each known way
   This way is my own way

153

You're the sail of my love boat
You're the captain and crew
You will always be
My necessity
I'd be lost without you

You're the cream in my coffee
You're the salt in my stew
You will always be
My necessity
I'd be lost without you

You're the starch in my collar
You're the lace in my shoe
You will always be
My necessity
I'd be lost without you!

(BUTCHER *finishes on a crescendo. A bounce from the band and the number ends. The pool of white spotlight slides off the* SINGER *and the band on to the floor. Claps from the dancers.*)

JEAN: Oh! It's ended.

BERNARD: It'll never end, my darling. Not for us.

(*They look at each other in the rather dim light, seemingly unaware that, around them, the other couples are leaving the dance floor.*)

JEAN: You really do forgive me, then?

BERNARD: There's nothing to forgive, Jean. It was my fault.

JEAN: No. I shouldn't have left you like that. (*Little giggle*) All alone with the cream cakes.

BERNARD: I could hardly bear to swallow. It was like chewing glue.

JEAN: We'll never do that to each other again. Will we, Bernard?

BERNARD: Never ever, my angel.

JEAN: Let's promise.

BERNARD: Yes. I promise!

JEAN: And me, too! I promise!

BERNARD: Oh, darling.

(*He gathers her into his arms. Neither of them seem to be aware that they are now completely alone in the middle of the still darkened dance*

Cream in My Coffee

floor. The big pool of white light slips around the interested and amused faces of the dancers at the little tables round the edge of the floor. Then slides mischievously across the floor—to settle in a sudden white blaze on BERNARD *and* JEAN *locked together in their kiss. They break apart, startled, embarrassed, blinking shyly in the light. The onlookers laugh and a few applaud.* JEAN *puts her hand to her face with a gasp.* BERNARD, *grinning, bashfully, leads her off the floor. The ballroom lights come up.*)

14. HOTEL SWIMMING POOL: 1938

BERNARD *is splashing about in the pool.* JEAN *is sunbathing on a lounger at the side of the pool.*

Further along the side of the pool, pretending to read a Zane Grey Western, JACK BUTCHER, *in white slacks, a striped blazer, and a long gin-and-lime, is covertly watching her.*

A wasp buzzes near JEAN. *She flaps at it in alarm, but it won't go away. Zzzz–zzzz–zzzzzzzzzz!*

JEAN: (*Frightened*) Oooh!

BUTCHER: (*Calls*) Don't hit at it! It'll go away then!

(JEAN *half rises in alarm as the wasp seems to dive-bomb her.*)

JEAN: (*Shriek*) Bernard!

(BERNARD *comes running, dripping.*)

BERNARD: What is it? Jean—?

JEAN: This wasp—oooh! No-o— Get off!

BERNARD: Keep still! Don't move—!

(JEAN *goes rigid with alarm. The wasp is on her shoulder.*)

JEAN: (*Faint*) Wh–Where is it?

BERNARD: On your shoulder. Keep still. It'll—

(*But she won't wait. With a cry of comical terror, she runs to the pool and makes a distinctly ungainly dive into the water.* BERNARD *starts to laugh and so does* BUTCHER.)

BUTCHER: That's the way. Drown the nasty little bleeder.

(BERNARD *stiffens slightly.*)

BERNARD: Are you all right, darling?

(JEAN *holds on to the side of the pool, still in the water.*)

JEAN: I can't stand bees and wasps and things, Bernard. I never could.

155

BERNARD: It's best not to hit out at them. They only sting
when they are attacked.

BUTCHER: That's what I told her.

(*Again,* BERNARD *frowns slightly, not wanting the familiarity.*)

JEAN: (*Smiles openly at* BUTCHER) I do make a fuss, don't I?

BUTCHER: Don't blame you, neither.

BERNARD: Jean—

JEAN: (*To* BUTCHER) Is it the broadcast tonight, Mr Butcher?

BUTCHER: *Mr* Butcher. *Mr* Butcher. What's all this? Has me hair
suddenly gone grey, little lady?

BERNARD: *My Wife* is simply being polite, Mr—ah—Butcher.

JEAN: Oh, Bernard. Don't sound so—*pompous.*

BERNARD: (*Annoyed*) I wasn't aware that I was, darling.

(*She pulls herself out of the pool.*)

JEAN: I've never met anyone who's sung on the wireless, Mr
Butcher.

BUTCHER: *Mr* Butcher. *Mr* Butcher.

BERNARD: Shall we get dressed, Jean? Or do you want another
swim?

JEAN: What time is it?

BUTCHER: (*Butting in again*) Five past four.

BERNARD: (*Irritated*) Hickory dickory dock.

JEAN: What's the matter, Bernard?

BERNARD: Come on. Let's go back to our room.

JEAN: Are you angry or something?

BERNARD: (*Rather testily*) Of course not!

(BUTCHER *resumes reading, or half reading, his cowboy book.*)

JEAN: I can't help it about wasps. It's always been the same.

(BERNARD *puts a towel around her shoulders.*)

BERNARD: It's not the wasps, my love. It's the wolves.

(BUTCHER *frowns into his book.*)

JEAN: (*Giggles*) Oh. You *are* silly.

(*They are walking away from the pool, towards the hotel.*)

BUTCHER: By—ee.

(*A remark mostly delivered to himself. We move with the young
couple, and our eyes are drawn on ahead to the big, white palace of
an hotel.*)

15. SUITE 343: 1938
The telephone rings, rings in an empty room. The curtains shift and seem to sigh at the half-open windows.

16. LONG, WIDE PASSAGE, HOTEL: 1938
BERNARD *and* JEAN, *in their draped towels, swimming costumes, etc., walking down the almost 'endless' corridor to their suite.*

A breeze has got up and at the half-open windows all along one side of the corridor the wooden toggles on the ends of the curtain-pulls are click–click–clicking against the window frames, behind and ahead of them.

Click–click–click: oddly ominous, insistent.

BERNARD: What a strange sound.

JEAN: It's the little wooden things on the end of—

BERNARD: Oh, I know what it *is*. It's just—
   (*He all but shivers.*)

JEAN: What is it, Bernard?

BERNARD: I dunno. (*Laughs uneasily.*) The strangest feeling.

JEAN: What sort of feeling? What do you mean?

BERNARD: I don't *mean* anything—just—oh, I'm being silly. A
   sort of—premonition.

JEAN: (*Slightly concerned*) But of what?
   (*He looks sideways at her, then takes her hand, a little too urgently.*)

BERNARD: You love me, don't you?

JEAN: Of course I do!

BERNARD: And I love you!

JEAN: Bernard—what's the matter?
   (*But they have arrived at the outer door of their suite.* BERNARD
   *throws off whatever faint, unlocatable unease or melancholy had
   momentarily fallen upon him.*)

BERNARD: (*Laugh*) Does it make you think there's something
   wrong with me when I say I love you?

JEAN: Don't be silly! There'd be something wrong with *me* if you
   didn't.
   (*He opens the door. They go through to—*)

157

17. SITTING ROOM, SUITE 343: 1938
The telephone has stopped ringing.

> BERNARD *looks at* JEAN, *speculatively.*

BERNARD: Darling—?

JEAN: (*Knowing what's coming*) Ye–es?

BERNARD: Shall we hang the notice on the door?

JEAN: (*Mock ignorance*) What notice is that, Bernard?

BERNARD: Do Not—um—um— (*Lets his jaw drop like an idiot*) — Dis–turb. Yeh. (*In mimic 'working class'*) Do—Not—Disturb. (*She responds in mimic 'working class', as in their ignorance they think it is.*)

JEAN: 'Ooo yew are greedy.

> (*They laugh. Then grow serious.*)

BERNARD: Shall I?

> (*She gives a quick, bright, eager nod.*)

JEAN: Yes, please, Mr Wilsher.

> (*An echo of Jack Butcher comes to him.*)

BERNARD: *Mr* Wilsher. *Mr* Wilsher.

> (*She giggles.*)

He doesn't—um—*appeal* to you does he, that Jew-boy?

JEAN: Is he Jewish?

BERNARD: Oh, they all are, aren't they. Singers and band leaders and that lot. (*Looks at her.*) But he *doesn't*—does he?

JEAN: Of course not! Silly!

> (BERNARD *looks at her, slightly anxious, then rushes to turn the 'Do Not Disturb' sign from the inside to the outside of the door. He comes swiftly back to her, and beats on his bare chest.*)

BERNARD: Me Tar–zan. You Jane.

JEAN: ('*Common*') Jean, ducky.

BERNARD: Oh, that'll make a nice change!

> (*He lifts her up in his arms and, as she laughs, carries her into the adjoining bedroom, making jungle noises.*
> *In the now empty room, the curtains sigh and sough at the half-open window. Outside, gulls cry, peculiarly sharp and plangent.*
> *The telephone goes. Ring—ring—*
> *A shout of protest from* BERNARD *in the bedroom, off.*
> *Ring–ring–ring. It stops. Then it starts again.*)

BERNARD *comes in, pulling bath towel or similar around himself.*
Ring–ring–ring.)
(*Snarl*) Spoil-sport! (*Picks up phone.*) Hello? (*His expression
changes.*) Yes, it's me. I mean, it is I. Uncle Geoffrey?
(*Pause.*) *What?* (*Huge sense of shock*) What? No—I can't take
it in. I can't—I— Yes. Oh, my God. Oh, dear God. I—
Yes, Uncle Geoff. Of course I'll come. Straightaway. At
once. (*His voice breaks.*) Is Mother all right—? Oh, my God.
Oh—I— (*Pulls himself together.*) Thank you for finding me,
Uncle. Thank you very much. I'll look up the trains and
come immediately. Goodbye. And—yes. Goodbye.
(*He puts the phone down and turns to look at* JEAN, *who has come to
the doorway, an anxious look on her face.*)
JEAN: Bernard?
BERNARD: It's my father, Jean. He— (*Gulp.*) He's been killed.

18. THE RAILWAY STATION: 1938
Summer evening.

    BERNARD *and* JEAN *sitting on a bench on the platform.*
    Beyond them, sound of stationary steam train, hissing and sighing.
    *She has both hands around one of his hands. He is stiff and tense, now
much more like the older Bernard.*
JEAN: But I think it's my *place* to be with you. Can't you see
    that?
BERNARD: How many times must I tell you that you were not,
    not, *not* supposed to be on holiday with me.
JEAN: Yes, Bernard, but in the circumstances—
BERNARD: Especially in the circumstances! What do you think
    my poor mother would feel—
JEAN: Doesn't she *like* me, Bernard?
BERNARD: Of course she does!
JEAN: But she doesn't think I'm good enough for you.
    (BERNARD *grits his teeth like the older Bernard is prone to do.*)
BERNARD: Jean, Jean. Will you stop talking like this.
JEAN: I know she doesn't. I *feel* it. I can tell!
BERNARD: What a time for you to be talking like this. Dear God
    above.

JEAN: Just because I didn't get my School Cert.

BERNARD: Jean. You are being very, very stupid.

JEAN: (*Near tears*) I know that's what you think about me. I know you think I haven't got any brains.

(*He sighs, trying to be patient.*)

BERNARD: Listen, my love. How would you be supposed to know about Father's—accident? Mmm?

JEAN: That's not the—

BERNARD: You're supposed to be camping in the Lake District, aren't you? With Gillian and her bloody horsey Girl Guides.

JEAN: Yes, but—

BERNARD: Nowhere near a telephone.

JEAN: I just thought I ought to be with you at a time like this.

BERNARD: Mother doesn't want any more shocks, does she? I don't want her to think you're *that* kind of—

(*He just manages to stop in time: but it is too late for her—*)

JEAN: (*Stiffening*) But I'm not that kind of girl, Bernard.

BERNARD: I didn't mean—

JEAN: Oh yes you did! You think I'm fast, don't you!

BERNARD: I think I'd better get on the train.

JEAN: I should never have agreed to come with you. (*The tears are coming.*) I won't even be able to marry in white, will I?

BERNARD: I wish to God you'd shut up. I really do. Can't you think of what I'm going through?

JEAN: I should have stayed a virgin. My mother said so. No man respects a woman who lets him have what he wants! All the girls say so . . . (*Choke.*)

BERNARD: You wanted to come, didn't you?

JEAN: (*Tears*) Only because— Only because you kept on about it—

BERNARD: Stop crying! Control yourself!

JEAN: I'm sorry—I can't—help it—

BERNARD: I'll have to get on the train.

JEAN: Will you come back? Do I have to stay?

BERNARD: Stay until Tuesday. I'll see what's what and—(*Swallow*) —the funeral—all that—and if I can

160

come back for the last couple of days—
(*He stands up, gripping his suitcase.*)
You've got enough money, Jean. I'll ring you every day.
JEAN: You won't. (*Sniffle.*) I know you won't—
BERNARD: Not if you're like *this* I won't!
(*Which shuts her up somewhat. He goes to the carriage. At the open door—*)
JEAN: You do love me, don't you? You still love me—?
BERNARD: Of course I do, silly.
(*They kiss. Down platform* GUARD *shouts.*)
GUARD: Close all doors! Close all doors!
JEAN: (*Wail*) Oh, Bernard!
(*He gets in, leans out of the train window.*)
BERNARD: I'll ring you every day. I'll ring every hour!
JEAN: Do you forgive me?
BERNARD: There's nothing to forgive—
(*They kiss. He is on the train, she on the platform. Whistle from* GUARD. *Huge woompf-wuff-hiss from train as it starts to leave platform.* BERNARD *and* JEAN *break apart at the last possible moment.*)
JEAN: Bernard. Oh, Bernard!
BERNARD: Jean— Be good!
(*Wave–wave–wave. Puff–puff–puff.*)

19. SEASIDE PIER: 1979
Discover elderly BERNARD *and* JEAN, *wrapped up against a brisk sea breeze, sitting facing the sea two-thirds of the way along a girdered and now decaying Victorian pier.*

Waves washing and thumping against the struts. Old people sitting aimlessly, looking out to sea. A few younger people walking up and down.

A MAN *at the head of some steps going down from the pier rails is touting business for his 'speed boat'.*
TOUT: Few more! Just a few more places for the next trip! Come aboard *Salty Anne* and speed round the harbour! Few more! Just a few more places!
JEAN: It's not very warm is it? For the time of year.
BERNARD: I've got a pain.

161

JEAN: Oh, dear.

BERNARD: In my chest.

JEAN: Is it bad?

BERNARD: Indigestion, I think.

JEAN: Do you want to go?

BERNARD: (*Snort*) Where to?

JEAN: Well—I don't see much point in sitting here. It isn't very comfortable.

BERNARD: I like looking at the sea.

JEAN: Yes.

(*Pause.*)

TOUT: (*Off*) Five more minutes! Few more places on *Salty Anne!* Come aboard!

JEAN: We can see the sea from our room. And it's a sight more comfortable.

BERNARD: I like the fresh air.

JEAN: (*Sigh*) Yes.

BERNARD: We can pretend we're waiting for a boat.

JEAN: We can even go on one, if you like.

BERNARD: Ah. But you don't know what sort of boat I mean.

(*He says this with an almost malicious glint.*)

JEAN: What sort of boat, Bernard?

BERNARD: The one we're waiting for.

JEAN: But we aren't . . .

BERNARD: (*Steadily*) I don't know why we bother to speak to each other. I simply don't know why we don't sit in silence. You never understand what I am talking about. Your head is full of cotton wool.

JEAN: Don't talk to me, then.

BERNARD: We *are* waiting for a boat. We are! You stupid old woman.

JEAN: Yes, dear. All right. If you like to think so. A trip in a boat would be very nice.

(*Pause. Then he looks at her, rather sadly.*)

BERNARD: I think it would be very very nice indeed. Except that I shall go on board well before you do. I'm not very kind, I know, but I shall still expect you to wave from the shore.

162

(*Now she understands what he means.*)

JEAN: Oh. *That* sort of boat—

BERNARD: Congratulations! It really is like watching the penny
drop.

JEAN: Why are you so—nasty? What have I done?

(*He doesn't answer. They both look out to sea.*)

TOUT: (*Shout*) Any more for the *Salty Anne!* Any more for the
speed boat! Any more for the boat!

20. HOTEL: 1938

*Sound of band in ballroom, and lights splashing out into summer's
night.*

21. LONG, WIDE CORRIDOR, HOTEL: 1938

Young JEAN, *alone, walks along the corridor to her room. She is upset.*

A young hotel WAITER *passes her, carrying tray with emptied
champagne bottle and two used champagne glasses. He looks at her as he
draws level.*

WAITER: Good evening, Miss.

(*But she doesn't even seem to see him. Her head lower and lower she
walks on to room 343. Faint sounds from the band drifting up from
the ballroom.*)

22. HOTEL BALLROOM: 1938

JACK BUTCHER *is singing. The band is playing.*

BUTCHER: (*Sings*) Somewhere the sun is shining
   So honey don't you cry
   We'll find a silver lining
   The clouds will soon roll by

   I hear a robin singing
   Upon a treetop high
   To you and me he's singing
   The clouds will soon roll by.

Cream in My Coffee

23. SUITE 343: 1938
Alone in the sitting room, restless, JEAN *stubs out a half-smoked cigarette, turns on wireless, and while it warms up goes to the window to look out at the darkly glistening sea.*

Radio comes on.

BUTCHER: (*Sings, on radio*) Each little tear and sorrow
      Only brings you closer to me
      Just wait until tomorrow
      What a happy day that will be

      Down lovers' lane together
      We'll wander you and I
      Goodbye to stormy weather
      The clouds will soon roll by.
      (*As the band bounces on,* JEAN *crosses the room, switches the wireless off, stands for a moment, then puts both her hands to her face as she bursts into tears. The picture fades.*)

24. LARGE SUBURBAN HOUSE: 1938
Early morning feel. Birds singing. Postman delivering letters. Dog barking from within the house.

But the curtains are shut at every window.

25. A DOWNSTAIRS ROOM IN THE HOUSE: 1938
Morning light trickling in a thin gruel under and at the sides of the closed curtains.

In the strange half-light a woman in her late fifties, MRS WILSHER, *sits half awake in a high-backed chair. She is herself very straight backed, a slender, severe lady with steel hair, steel eyes, steel demeanour.*

Eventually, we see in the room an ornate coffin, its lid unscrewed.

Tap, tap on the door. A little uncertain.

Young BERNARD *comes in, bearing a cup of tea. He is clearly just a little nervous of his mother.*

BERNARD: Mother?

MRS WILSHER: Good morning, Bernard.

    (BERNARD *darts a quick, nervous look at the coffin.*)

BERNARD: Good morning, Mother. I've brought you a cup of tea.

Cream in My Coffee

MRS WILSHER: That's very kind of you.

BERNARD: I took it to your room. I didn't know where you— I could see your bed hadn't been slept in.

MRS WILSHER: You shouldn't go into my bedroom, Bernard.

BERNARD: No, I— Have you been sitting here all night, Mother?

MRS WILSHER: Yes, I have.

BERNARD: I'm sorry. I didn't know.

MRS WILSHER: I didn't wish for company.

BERNARD: No. But—aren't you going to drink your tea—?

MRS WILSHER: It's very nice, thank you.

(*But she makes no attempt to drink it.* BERNARD *stands in front of her, awkward.*)

BERNARD: Haven't you been to sleep at all?

MRS WILSHER: I don't think so. I hope I haven't.

BERNARD: Aren't you tired?

(*He looks again, quickly, uneasily at the coffin.*)

MRS WILSHER: (*Almost angrily*) Of course I am.

BERNARD: But— (*swallow*) —why did you—

MRS WILSHER: (*Cutting in*) Why? What do you mean—*why*?

BERNARD: You will only exhaust yourself. It doesn't help Fa—I'm sorry, Mother, but it doesn't help Father, does it?

MRS WILSHER: Oh. You're sure of that, are you? You know about these things, do you?

BERNARD: Yes, Mother. I'm sure.

MRS WILSHER: Mmm. Thought you might be.

(*He looks at her, half in wary affection, half exasperated.*)

BERNARD: I'm only trying to see that you get a proper rest. Why don't you drink your tea? It's getting cold.

MRS WILSHER: There are worse things in life than cold tea.

BERNARD: Shall I open the curtains for you?

MRS WILSHER: No!

BERNARD: Well—all right—but shouldn't you have some more light in here?

MRS WILSHER: (*Gentler*) No. Thank you.

(*He again glances swiftly at the coffin.*)

Go and look.

BERNARD: What?

165

MRS WILSHER: Go and look at your father's face. It is quite unmarked. And very peaceful.

BERNARD: (*Uneasily*) I'd—I'd rather not . . .

MRS WILSHER: Oh. You'd rather not. Why is that? Why would you 'rather not'?

BERNARD: I'd rather remember him as he—when (*slight stutter*) when he was alive.

MRS WILSHER: Sit down, Bernard.

BERNARD: What?

MRS WILSHER: Sit yourself down.

(*Reluctant, and a bit like a child about to be scolded, he does as he is told, but making sure that he sits out of view of the coffin.*)

BERNARD: (*In a near gabble*) I can't help it, I don't like it. I just don't— I can't bear to be in here like this, in the dark, with the coffin and—it's morbid. I think it's *morbid*.

MRS WILSHER: (*Faint smile*) Have you finished?

BERNARD: (*Subdued*) Yes.

MRS WILSHER: Did you love your father, Bernard?

BERNARD: I—he was a very *gentle* man. And sensitive.

MRS WILSHER: But did you love him?

BERNARD: Of course I did! Really, Mother, the way you put things.

MRS WILSHER: He was a nice man, your father.

BERNARD: (*As though arguing*) Yes! He was!

MRS WILSHER: Very nice.

(*In her mouth it sounds close to an accusation. He stares at her, waiting for more. It doesn't come so—*)

BERNARD: (*Miserably*) Very nice indeed.

MRS WILSHER: And weak.

(BERNARD *drops his head. He is finding this all too horrible for words.*)

BERNARD: I don't think—

MRS WILSHER: (*Sharply*) What's that? I can't hear you.

(BERNARD *looks up, tears in his eyes.*)

BERNARD: I don't think you can hear many people, Mother. You don't hear them because you don't listen to them.

MRS WILSHER: Umph. Most of them haven't got anything worth saying.

BERNARD: That's what you thought about Father.

(*This shuts her up momentarily. They sit in silence. He looks at her, warily, and cautiously wipes his eyes with the back of his hand.*)

MRS WILSHER: Why do you think I have sat here all night? Why do you think I have kept vigil?

BERNARD: Because you— (*Shakes his head, numbly*) —because . . . (*He stops.*)

MRS WILSHER: Because in thinking about your father and his life I was thinking about you, Bernard, and your life.
(*He finds this rather menacing.*)

BERNARD: In—in what way? I mean—well. Yes. Thank you.

MRS WILSHER: And I also wanted to pay penance.

BERNARD: Sorry?

MRS WILSHER: There are especial times in one's life—in *everyone's* life—when one has a positive moral obligation to take stock of one's self and one's direction.

BERNARD: Yes, Mother. (*Comically clears his throat.*) Absolutely.

MRS WILSHER: Or relatively.

BERNARD: What?

MRS WILSHER: You said 'absolutely', I said 'relatively'.

BERNARD: Oh. Well—yes. Quite.
(MRS WILSHER *sighs heavily, as though in despair at his timidity.*)

MRS WILSHER: Sometimes, you know, your boldness really bowls me over.

BERNARD: Look here, Mother . . . this is neither the time nor the place to—
(*But she darts in a quick interruption.*)

MRS WILSHER: How was the seaside?
(*He sits bolt upright, like one suddenly aware of great danger.*)

BERNARD: Oh. Well. Not too bad, actually. Quite nice, really.

MRS WILSHER: Strange place to go on one's own though, isn't it?

BERNARD: (*Swallow*) —I don't know. No. Not really. Plenty of—um—plenty of things to do.

MRS WILSHER: Like fornicating, do you mean?

BERNARD: Mother!

MRS WILSHER: I'm very disappointed in you.
(*Flustered,* BERNARD *lurches to his feet, trying to make himself storm out.*)

167

BERNARD: You always have been. That's the trouble. And you were always disappointed in Father, too. Don't sit here with his coffin telling me—

MRS WILSHER: (*Rising tone*) Sit down please, Bernard. I haven't finished.

(BERNARD, *upset, makes a melodramatic gesture towards the coffin.*)

BERNARD: No! But *he* has!

(MRS WILSHER *grips the arm of her chair but keeps control.*)

MRS WILSHER: Sit down, Bernard. I want you to sit down.

BERNARD: No!

(*But he does not go. And then he suddenly seems to give way.*)

MRS WILSHER: (*Quite gently*) Don't upset yourself, my dear. Please do as I ask. Please do as I ask. Please sit down, Bernard.

(*Like a lamb, he does as he is told.*)

BERNARD: Yes, Mother. I'm sorry.

MRS WILSHER: You've always been a good boy to me. You've always understood me.

(*He shakes his head dumbly.*)

BERNARD: I— (*Sigh*) Yes, Mother.

MRS WILSHER: That girl will not do, Bernard. She simply will—not—do.

BERNARD: Why do you say that? Why?

MRS WILSHER: Oh, she's a pretty little thing, no one can deny.

BERNARD: (*Between his teeth*) She's beautiful!

MRS WILSHER: You are so malleable. So easily persuaded. So very much like your poor father.

BERNARD: I love her. And I am going to marry her.

MRS WILSHER: Did she persuade you to take this—holiday together? Bernard?

BERNARD: We had separate rooms.

MRS WILSHER: I'm very sorry to have to say that that is not true. Your uncle was first told that 'Mr and Mrs Wilsher' were not in their room.

BERNARD: Mother. I'm 26 years old. And this is 1938.

MRS WILSHER: Go and look at your father.

BERNARD: What?

MRS WILSHER: Go and look into his face, Bernard.

BERNARD: I'd really rather not.

MRS WILSHER: It's the face of a man at peace, Bernard.

BERNARD: I hope so—

MRS WILSHER: At peace.

BERNARD: Yes, Mother . . .

(*Little pause.*)

MRS WILSHER: Is it your intention to disturb his spirit?

(BERNARD *stares at her.*)

BERNARD: What did you say?

MRS WILSHER: Are you going to marry a little flibbertigibbet from the Post Office and turn your back on your own inheritance?

BERNARD: (*Steadily*) I don't want to offend you. That's the last thing in the world I want. But I *do* have my own life to make in the way that *I* think best. I'm not very brave, Mother, and I'm not very clever, but— (*His voice lets him down: it suddenly breaks.*) —I shall miss Father's money much, much less than I shall miss *him*—

(*He suddenly starts to cry.* MRS WILSHER *says nothing but she purses her lips. He stops crying, wipes his eyes, then, unexpectedly, goes over to the coffin. He braces himself, then looks down at his father's face.*)

TOUT: (*Off*) Any more for the boat! The boat is leaving now!

26. ON THE PIER: 1979

Here, old BERNARD*'s face is so similar to the face in the ornate coffin.*

TOUT: (*Off*) Come on, now. Nice trip round the bay. The boat is about to leave. Any more for the boat!

JEAN: It isn't very warm, Bernard. Can't we go back now?

BERNARD: What?

JEAN: I'm cold. I feel cold.

BERNARD: (*Sigh*) Yes. So do I.

(*They look out on the now grey sea. Drift away across the waters towards the black smudge of a distant ship or yacht. Slowly bring up—*)

SINGER: You're the cream in my coffee
You're the salt in my stew

You will always be
My necessity
I'd be lost without you.

27. THE GRAND SEASIDE HOTEL: 1979
The hotel WAITERS *are gathering in chairs and loungers from around the swimming pool: another summer's day is drawing to a close. Bright lights splashing out from the great white palace.*

One of the chair-clearing waiters suddenly flaps his arm. There is a wasp buzzing round him. The other laughs.

28. THE VAST ENTRANCE HALL, HOTEL: 1979
GUESTS—*preponderantly middle-aged or elderly, but with some young couples—are crossing from the dining room to the lounges, where a* TRIO *of musicians (all that is left now of the once big bands) are thrashing out standards.*

'Smoke Gets in Your Eyes'—with an electronic attachment on the piano, a trumpet, and a double-bass.

29. HOTEL DINING ROOM: 1979
A WAITER *at a small spirit stove is making crêpes Suzette in the pan. He flames it with an almost wearily disdainful flourish. And we see that he is doing it for elderly* BERNARD *and* JEAN.

JEAN, *who has long been frustrated in her natural, warm interest in practically any human activity, watches the final flourish in the pan, with bright eyes.* BERNARD *simply waits.*

WAITER: Here we are, madam—I hope you enjoy it.

JEAN: (*Beam*) Oh, I'm sure I shall.

(BERNARD *watches it being spooned on to her plate.*)

BERNARD: I hope it's better than the main course, that's all I can say.

JEAN: (*Apologetically*) My husband suffers from dyspepsia. (*Looks at* WAITER.) Indigestion.

WAITER: (*Uninterested*) Oh, dear. Such a pity.

BERNARD: I can see how very concerned you are. Breaks your warm Italian heart, doesn't it?

WAITER: Sir?

BERNARD: (*Snarl*) Never mind. Get on with it.

WAITER: (*Filling* BERNARD's *plate*) I hope you enjoy it, sir.

BERNARD: (*With bad grace*) Thank you.

JEAN: (*Compensating*) Thank you!

(*The* WAITER *moves away, glad to leave this particular table.* JEAN *drops her head, and pushes the food around her plate, miserable. He eats, chews. Self-absorbed, grumpily so. Sounds of 'Yesterday' (Lennon–McCartney) drifting through from the lounge.* JEAN *looks up from her plate, and looks steadily at her husband. He is unaware of her scrutiny.*)

JEAN: (*Eventually*) 'Yesterday'.

(*He stops chewing.*)

BERNARD: What?

JEAN: They're playing 'Yesterday'.

(*He stares at her as though she were a cretin.*)

BERNARD: What?

JEAN: The band. They're playing 'Yesterday'.

BERNARD: Umph.

(*He carries on eating, ignoring her. She continues to stare at him. He gradually becomes aware of her scrutiny.*)

What are you looking at me like that for?

JEAN: A cat can look at the Queen.

BERNARD: The astonishing originality of your remarks sometimes takes my breath away.

JEAN: I wish they would.

BERNARD: (*Snort*) You wish they would what. . . ?

JEAN: Take your breath away.

(*He frowns. There is an ambiguity in the remark he wishes to clear up.*)

BERNARD: Literally, do you mean? Kill me, do you mean?

(*She looks at him, then smiles sweetly.*)

JEAN: Of course not, dear.

30. BALLROOM: 1938

On the bandstand, bootblack-haired JACK BUTCHER *goes crescendo on the last lines of his most popular song.*

BUTCHER: (*Sings*) . . . You will always be

> My necessity
> I'd be lost without you!
> (*And a concluding bounce or two from the dinner-jacketed band as sharp-eyed* JACK *swiftly surveys his audience. His eyes settle and gleam. He has seen—*)

31. TABLE, EDGE OF DANCE FLOOR: 1938
Where young JEAN *sits alone with her cocktail, a 'poor lonely me' look on her otherwise pert face. She claps mournfully, about twice. Then sees* BUTCHER *crossing the floor, obviously coming to her. She sort of 'composes' herself.*

BUTCHER: Hell–o. All on your own–i–o little lady?

JEAN: I—yes.

BUTCHER: Did you like the song?

JEAN: Yes. It was very nice.

BUTCHER: Want a drink?

JEAN: I—no. I'd better not. Thank you.
  (*But he sits down at her table.*)

BUTCHER: Mind if I park myself?

JEAN: It seems you already have.

BUTCHER: But do you mind?

JEAN: (*Faint hesitation*) No.

BUTCHER: A pretty girl like you shouldn't be all on her lonesome.

JEAN: *My husband* was called away.

BUTCHER: Oh.

JEAN: On business.

BUTCHER: What business is that? (*Sees her expression.*) If I may stick my hooter in. Honk! Honk!

JEAN: (*Laugh*) The retail business.

BUTCHER: The little corner shop, you mean?

JEAN: (*Snooty*) No. I don't. Wilsher Stores as a matter of fact.
  (BUTCHER *gives a vulgar little whistle.*)

BUTCHER: In which case, you can buy me a drink.

JEAN: (*Uncertain*) Do—do you want one?

BUTCHER: (*Laugh*) I'm only pulling your leg, Mrs—Wilsher. Is it?

JEAN: Y–Yes.

172

(*Something about the way she replies gives him a quickly stifled 'A–
Ah' expression.*)

BUTCHER: I came across to talk to you because you looked kinda
sad.

(*Her eyes immediately glisten with swift, unshed tears.*)

JEAN: I—I shouldn't have come, really.

BUTCHER: What? And missed the vocal refrain?

JEAN: I've made a mistake.

(*He looks at her with a glint.*)

BUTCHER: We all do that, don't we?

JEAN: (*Barely audible*) Yes.

(*He waits. She lowers her head. Then he suddenly takes her hand, on
top of the table.*)

BUTCHER: Why don't you tell Uncle all about it, eh?

JEAN: (*Stiffening*) No . . . oh, no. I can't.

BUTCHER: A trouble shared is a trouble halved. That's what I've
always found, believe you me.

JEAN: Please let go of my hand.

BUTCHER: Aw, now.

JEAN: Please!

(*And she pulls her hand away.*)

32. LONG HOTEL CORRIDOR: 1979

Old BERNARD *and* JEAN *returning to their suite after their
less-than-amiable dinner.*

*The long, wide corridor seems to stretch ahead of them in apparently
endless perspective. The night breeze has got up and, as before, strangely
ominous, the little wooden toggles at the end of the curtain-pulls are going
click–click–click in the current of air from the partly opened windows.*

Pad–shuffle–pad as BERNARD, *in particular, shuffles away.
Click–click–click. And* BERNARD *stops.*

JEAN: What's the matter? Are you short of breath again?

BERNARD: That noise.

JEAN: What noise? Oh—it's the wooden handles against the
window frames.

BERNARD: (*Obscurely disturbed*) It makes me feel—I don't know—

JEAN: What? It makes you feel what?

BERNARD: I have been here before.

JEAN: But you *have* been here before.

.BERNARD: No, no. Like a—you know, like a taste at the back of your throat or like something just out of your reach—something— oh, never mind. But it's not a nice feeling, that's what I *do* know.

JEAN: Come on, dear. Let's not stop here in the corridor. I want to go to the bathroom.

BERNARD: I feel like a brandy.

JEAN: You can ring room service.

BERNARD: It would be nice to get drunk again, wouldn't it? Well and truly pickled.

JEAN: Better not.

BERNARD: (*Petulant*) Why 'better not'? God Almighty.

JEAN: You must please yourself, dear.

(*As they move on—*)

BERNARD: I shall! I bloody shall!

(*Seen from behind, they journey slowly along the endless corridor, like characters in a dream. The click–click–click of the toggles starting to dominate. Click–click–click.*)

33. CHURCHYARD: 1938

The burial of Bernard's father—the concluding 'Earth to earth, ashes to ashes', etc., of the sonorously beautiful Anglican service.

The clergyman intoning. Faces at the graveside.

Young BERNARD *is standing next to his formidable* MOTHER.

The clergyman's voice fades under the voice of old BERNARD, *talking to old* JEAN *on the pier.*

OLD BERNARD: I don't know why we bother to speak to each other. I simply don't know why we don't sit in silence. You never understand what I am talking about. Your head is full of cotton wool.

(*Earth clunking down on the coffin. The relatives file past the grave, and look down into it, dropping flowers.*)

OLD JEAN: Don't talk to me, then.

(*As* BERNARD *files past grave—*)

OLD BERNARD: (*Snarl*) We *are* waiting for a boat. We are! You stupid old woman.

OLD JEAN: Yes, dear. All right. If you like to think so. A trip
in a boat would be very nice.
(*The huddled mourners are now seen in a perspective of stone angels,
marble slabs and Celtic crosses, slowly breaking from the formality
of the ceremony.*)

OLD BERNARD: I think it would be very nice indeed. Except that
I shall go on board well before you do. I'm not very kind, I
know, but I shall still expect you to wave from the shore.
(*At the graveside, isolated in mood from the other mourners, young
BERNARD's face is tense and blanched with grief and anxiety. The
song (dance band) 'Cream in My Coffee' swells up, as though from
the graveside ceremony.*)

34. HOTEL CORRIDOR: 1938
Late. Corridor empty.
   *The weird click–click–click from the windows, the length of the long
corridor.*
   Then, unexpectedly, the gurgle of a young woman's laughter.
   And we suddenly discover young JEAN, *the worse for drink, leaning all
over sharp-faced* JACK BUTCHER, *very much in control of himself, as the
pair meander back to Jean's room.*

JEAN: (*Giggle, loudly*) Ooooh—I'm squiffy, Jack—I'm really
squiffy—
   (BUTCHER *is glancing about.*)
BUTCHER: Shh! Not so loud, angel.
JEAN: (*With abandon*) Why not! I'm—shh! Yesh. Shhh!
BUTCHER: There's a good little girl.
   (*He steers her skilfully along the corridor.*)
JEAN: Thash what I am I am. That's—shh! *Shhh!*
BUTCHER: (*Urgently*) Where's the key?
JEAN: (*Giggle*) What? What?
BUTCHER: The key! The key to your room. Where is it, angel? In
your bag. Come on. Come on—
   (*She drunkenly puts one finger on his chest.*)
JEAN: Naughty, naughty.
BUTCHER: You've got to open the door, darling, entcha?
JEAN: (*Sways*) Oooh. Bad boy. Bad bad boy!

BUTCHER: (*Controlling exasperation*) But you can't walk straight fru the bleedin' door, now, canya bab–ee!

JEAN: (*Giggles*) You're not coming in! You—musn't come in—

BUTCHER: 'Course not. *I* know that, don't I?

JEAN: That's all right, then. (*Drunkenly*) That's all—fine and dandy. . . !

(*Fumbling in her bag, she drops the key to the floor.*)

BUTCHER: Oops-a-daisy.

(*And he picks up the key.*)

JEAN: I'm—I feel—ooh. All funny.

(*He opens the door.*)

BUTCHER: (*Worried*) Eh, now. Don't pass out on me, now.

JEAN: (*Giggle*) Don't be silly—!

(*He pulls—literally pulls—her through the door. A moment. Then* BUTCHER*'s hand emerges to hang the 'Do Not Disturb' sign on the door handle.*)

35. THE LITTLE HALLWAY, SUITE 343: 1938

JEAN *has propped herself drunkenly against the wall. And her eyes are rolling a bit.*

BUTCHER: My, my. You *are* in a state entcha honey?

(*Always a curious combination of pseudo-American and cockney.*)

JEAN: I'm—I want to—oh, God—

BUTCHER: You'd better lie on the bed before you fall down. Where is it? Eh? Oh, yeh—through here. C'mon, darling. Rest your tootsies.

(*He tries to lift her up.*)

JEAN: No.

(*He kisses her.*)

(*Mumble, mumble*) No, no.

(*He kisses her again, very hungrily, pawing at her. She giggles.*)

BUTCHER: Atta girl.

JEAN: The— (*Hiccup*) —the cream in my coffee.

(*He half takes, half carries her through to the bedroom.*)

BUTCHER: No—the salt in my stew.

(*He pushes the bedroom door shut with his foot. We are left outside the bedroom door. The music swells.*)

36. SITTING ROOM, SUITE 343: 1938

Morning. The room is empty. Sound of gulls crying and screaming outside. The telephone starts to ring. Ring–ring.

A startled, dishevelled, virtually naked and hungover JEAN *emerges at the sitting-room doorway. She looks at the ringing telephone, eyes widening, scared. Then makes herself go across the room and pick it up.*

JEAN: H–Hello . . . Bernard! (*She bursts into tears.*) Oh, Bernard! Bernard! I'm so— (*Sob*) —Oh, Bernard. Why did you leave me here. . . ?

37. A ROOM IN BERNARD'S HOME: 1938

BERNARD *on the telephone.*

BERNARD: No, Jean, no—don't cry. Don't cry, my love. I want you to listen to me. No. Jean—please don't cry so hard— Jean? My father was buried yesterday afternoon—Jean? Please. No. Listen to me.

Yes, I know. I shouldn't have left you on your own.

—Jean? Why are you so upset? Listen—I've been awake all night, thinking about things—about what sort of person I am—about what I really want—about *you.*

Most of all about you.

Jean? Are you listening—?

38. SUITE 343: 1938

JEAN, *her face streaked with tears, tries to compose her juddering sobs.*

JEAN: (*Gulp*) Yes—Bernard—yes. I'm listening. Oh, Bernard—I love you. I love you so. And—yes. I'm listening. (*Crying*) I *am* listening—

39. THE ROOM IN BERNARD'S HOME: 1938

BERNARD: I'm coming back just as soon as I—

I'm not going to wait until September— I saw the vicar yesterday. After the funeral.

Jean—listen my love, my only darling, I asked him about publishing the banns—

Yes! I want us to marry as soon as we can—

177

40. THE HALL OUTSIDE BERNARD'S ROOM: 1938
MRS WILSHER, *ramrod straight, but expressionless, stands stock still outside the door, listening to* BERNARD *on the telephone.*
BERNARD: (*Off, on telephone*) Please don't cry so. Please my
darling. I know I've been weak. I know I've— But I want
to marry you. I want want want to share my life with you—
(MRS WILSHER *opens the door and walks straight in.*)

41. BERNARD'S ROOM: 1938
BERNARD: (*On telephone*) We won't be as well off as we had
thought and as you had the right to expect— No, Jean,
listen to *everything* I have to say—
(*He deliberately turns and faces his* MOTHER, *who stands staring at
him, still utterly expressionless.*)
You were absolutely right. My mother *doesn't* approve.
Jean?
But it's my life. And I don't want her to live it for me in
the same way that she did for Father.
I know that if I have to spend my days without *you* by my
side, then life for me would have no colour and no meaning
and no joy—
Jean? Don't cry, my poor darling.
I love you. And I want you to be my wife— (*His
expression changes.*) Jean? Are you there? Jean?
(*He looks at the phone.*)
Cut off.

42. SITTING ROOM, SUITE 343: 1938
JEAN *has put the phone down in the anguish of her shame and distress.*
JEAN: (*Wail*) Oh, Bern–ard!
(*She sinks on to the near settee and sobs without control.*)

43. THE BEACH: 1979
*A bright, calm day, with the tide rolling in and sparkles of reflected light
glittering in spangles on the sea. Gulls wheel and cry.*
*Pulling back from the actual shoreline—where children paddle—up the
gentle slope of the shingle where people sunbathe—to a couple of deckchairs*

almost up against the wall of the beach where it yields to steps up to the
first level of a beach promenade.

In the deck chairs, old BERNARD *and* JEAN. *He is wearing a large,*
old-fashioned straw hat which all but hides his face, and, ludicrously, his
trousers are rolled up to about mid-calf, his shoes and socks still on. JEAN,
head lolled back, is crinkling up her eyes in the sun.

Observe a while, then—

BERNARD: (*Suddenly*) I used to see her in the garden almost every
morning. In the school holidays.

JEAN: What?

BERNARD: Terribly overgrown. Grass up to your knees.
Brambles. Couldn't see the path in summer. Like
something out of the jungle.

JEAN: What are you talking about?

BERNARD: The old woman.

JEAN: What old woman?

BERNARD: The old woman with the cat!

JEAN: What cat—?

BERNARD: You're no sort of companion, are you? You never
listen to what I say!

JEAN: You must have been talking to yourself.

BERNARD: What do you mean? Talking to myself?
(*A little way down the beach, a* YOUTH *and his* GIRL *are lying*
together on a spread-out blanket. The YOUTH *tunes in to Radio One*
on a small transistor.)

JEAN: You suddenly said about seeing someone in the garden.

BERNARD: (*Comically testily*) Well I did! Nearly every morning!

JEAN: But you hadn't been talking about anybody, Bernard. I
can't read your mind, can I?

BERNARD: Puss! Puss!

JEAN: What?
(*The pop and prattle from the radio starts to irritate him.*)

BERNARD: The old woman with the cat!

JEAN: Oh. Yes. In the tumbledown little cottage.

BERNARD: I thought she was *hideously* old. When I was a boy.

JEAN: Well, children do, don't they?

BERNARD: It shouldn't be allowed!

179

JEAN: It's only natural, dear . . . children have such funny little ways . . .

BERNARD: That noise, I mean! That damned radio!

JEAN: Oh. Yes.

BERNARD: No consideration for other people. None whatsoever.

JEAN: (*Sigh*) Don't listen to it.

(*She just wants to sit in the sun.*)

BERNARD: But you *have* to listen to it! You can't switch your ears off. Bloody noise. (*Shouts at the* COUPLE) Hey!

JEAN: Don't—oh, don't, Bernard—

BERNARD: Hey! You, there!

(*But the young* COUPLE *do not turn.* JEAN *is scared that he is going to make a scene.*)

JEAN: Shall we move further along? There are plenty of chairs on over there—

BERNARD: Why should *we* move? Why should *we* be driven away?

JEAN: Don't make a scene, will you? Please, Bernard.

BERNARD: Why should *we* have to move?

JEAN: I think I'd like to go back to the hotel, anyway.

BERNARD: No you wouldn't. (*Shouts*) Hey!

JEAN: Yes, I would. Especially if you're going to make a scene.

BERNARD: (*Screams*) Hey! You! Yobbo! Switch it off!

(*Plenty of others pay him attention, but not the offending* YOUTH.)

JEAN: (*Distressed*) Please. Oh. Please don't.

(*But* BERNARD *is virtually grinding his teeth in one of his whirlwind rages.*)

BERNARD: Bloody ignorant selfish lout. Spoiling everybody's holiday. (*Shout*) Switch it off, you bugger!

(*It becomes apparent from a swift backward leer that the* YOUTH *has heard him. His response is to turn his radio up even louder.*)

JEAN: I'm going back . . . I'm not staying here . . .

(*She pulls herself out of the deckchair, with difficulty.*)

BERNARD: (*Snarl*) Sit down.

JEAN: No, Bernard. I'm going back.

BERNARD: (*Sudden, abrupt change*) No, no, Jean. Don't do that.

JEAN: You make me feel so embarrassed.

BERNARD: (*Puzzled frown*) Do I—? But—

JEAN: You let yourself down. You make a spectacle of yourself.

BERNARD: But we've had a *nice* holiday—haven't we? You've enjoyed yourself—haven't you?

JEAN: (*Hesitant*) Yes . . .

BERNARD: Sit down, then. Come on.

JEAN: I think I'd like to go back for a cup of tea or something.

BERNARD: My leg hurts.

JEAN: Does it?

BERNARD: I don't want to walk for a bit. Don't think I can.

JEAN: Then stop getting into one of your states.

BERNARD: Yes, dear.

JEAN: You promise?

BERNARD: (*Slightly grudging*) Yes. All right.

JEAN: We'll stay a bit longer then. But no more shouting.

(*She sits back down in the deckchair.* BERNARD *seems glad that she has sat down again. He is quiet. But then he suddenly glares at her venomously, and comically. She takes no notice. The radio still plays. Sensing from an inaudible movement of his lips that he is about to start again, she speaks—*)

What were you saying about the cat?

BERNARD: What? What cat?

JEAN: The old lady's cat.

(*A fraught moment while he works it out.*)

BERNARD: Oh. Yes.

JEAN: You didn't finish what you were saying.

BERNARD: Old Mrs Teague.

JEAN: Yes.

BERNARD: Near nigh every morning— 'Puss! Puss!' and this grisly old tom would come running from whatever place it was in the jungle. Mangy old thing. *Both* of them, in fact.

JEAN: You can get very attached to a cat.

BERNARD: (*Snort*) Attached. It was the only thing she would talk to. She was as mad as a hatter. Lived in absolute muddle and filth. I used to think she was a witch. And as old as the hills.

JEAN: How old was she?

BERNARD: (*Repeating himself*) I don't suppose she was a day older than I am now.

181

(*Pause. Which lengthens.*)

(*Eventually*) Several mornings in a row she called 'Puss! Puss!' in that horrible old croak of hers. And the cat didn't come running. It had disappeared.

JEAN: They are very independent.

BERNARD: Who are?

JEAN: Cats. (*Smile*) And old ladies.

BERNARD: Yes. And very much the same, too. These two were, anyway. An old witch and her mangy old tom-cat. I wish they'd turn that radio off!

JEAN: Take no notice.

BERNARD: Bloody hooligan!

JEAN: (*Quickly*) What happened to the cat?

BERNARD: The cat—yes. I saw her one morning. I shall never forget it, not as long as I live. She had come out as far as the broken-down old wall, looking for the cat. Then I saw her pick up this stiff dead thing from the long grass. It was the cat. Must have been dead for days.

JEAN: Oh, dear.

BERNARD: And do you know what she did? She kissed it and hugged it and kissed it. On the mouth, mind you. On its stinking mouth. Crying and wailing all the time.

JEAN: How horrible.

BERNARD: And then she suddenly tossed it aside. Threw it away. She stopped crying and kissing it and just threw it down in the grass like a sack of potatoes. And went back to the house as though nothing whatsoever had happened. I don't know why it made such a profound impression upon me, but it did.

JEAN: Yes. It's strange the things which stick in the mind, and those that don't. I was trying to remember my father's voice the other day—not his face, his *voice*—and do you know, I couldn't.

BERNARD: (*With relish*) He had a sort of Midlands whine.

JEAN: He didn't like *you* much, either.

(*The malicious smile dies on his face. Pause.*)

BERNARD: (*Sudden shout*) Switch it off!

182

Cream in My Coffee

44. HOTEL LOUNGE: 1938

Teatime. The STRING TRIO *are scraping happily through 'Roses of Picardy'.*

Young JEAN, *alone, but with the air of one nervously waiting, fiddles with her tea.*

From one of the doorways, JACK BUTCHER *comes in. Stands, looks around. She is looking at the main doorway, into the reception hall, and does not see him. He hesitates, then not too sure, but with smile glued on, goes across to her.*

BUTCHER: Good afternoon.

    (She starts, then quickly composes herself.)

JEAN: *(Severely)* What do you want?

BUTCHER: To see how you are. None the worse for wear, I sincerely hope.

JEAN: I think you've got an incredible *cheek.*

BUTCHER: Oh? Come on, now. I looked after you, didn't I?

JEAN: If you ever say anything about it to anybody, I'll—

BUTCHER: What sort of bloke do you think I am?

JEAN: Oh, I know what sort of bloke you are, all right. I just don't want you to talk about me to any of your—cronies. Not ever!

BUTCHER: Don't worry. I won't.

JEAN: Are you sure? Quite, quite sure?

BUTCHER: 'Course I won't. Scout's honour. *(Little pause.)* It was nice though, wasn't it?

JEAN: Please go away.

BUTCHER: You didn't need much encouragement, did you?

JEAN: I don't wish to talk about it.

BUTCHER: No. Well—no harm in thinking about it, though. Is there?

    (She sees BERNARD *arrive, and look about. She stiffens.)*

JEAN: Here's my husband! Go away! Quickly.

BUTCHER: *(Alarmed)* 'Ere! You won't *tell* him, will you?

JEAN: Not on your life.

    (She smiles and waves at BERNARD.)

BUTCHER: Toodle–oo then. Thanks for the memory.

    (And he scurries away, trying to look casual and dignified, but

Cream in My Coffee

failing to seem either. BERNARD *stands and looks and looks at her.*)
JEAN: (*Faintly*) Bernard. . . ?
BERNARD: Jean!
  (*And he rushes to her arms, but unfortunately trips on a fold in the carpet, sprawling headlong, and banging his mouth on the edge of the table.*)
JEAN: (*Shriek*) Bernard!
  (*He looks up at her, dazed, a puzzled smile on his face. Picture 'turns over' to—*)

45. GRAND HOTEL: 1979
The WAITERS *are gathering up chairs, loungers, glasses, etc., from around the pool as dusk thickens.*

46. HOTEL CORRIDOR: 1979
Again and again the wind stirs at the windows, moving the wooden toggles, click–click–click at the window frames, all along the long, wide passage.
  Old BERNARD *and* JEAN *appear in view, walking from their room towards the lifts. He is in dinner jacket, she in long evening dress.*
JEAN: Quite like old times, won't it be?
BERNARD: I don't expect so.
JEAN: The ballroom. A proper band. Oh, yes. It takes me back.
  (*They walk on. Click–click–click.*)
BERNARD: (*Suddenly*) I don't like it.
JEAN: What don't you like?
BERNARD: That noise!
  (*They walk on.*)

47. HALL OUTSIDE BALLROOM: 1979
Couples in dinner dress promenade or sit as though taking a break from the dancing inside.
  From the wide open huge double doors the sound of a dance band. And they are playing 'You're the Cream in My Coffee'.
  Oddly enough, too, the couples outside are all young, and the ladies are somehow dressed and coiffured as though for a 1930s' fancy dress.
  BERNARD *and* JEAN *arrive at the entrance.*

JEAN: (*Irritatingly repetitive*) Quite like old times!

BERNARD: Don't keep on. Don't keep saying that.

JEAN: Oh, Bernard. Why are you always so grumpy?
(*He doesn't answer. They move in through the double doors of the ballroom.*)

48. THE CHANDELIERED GRAND BALLROOM: 1979

It is bright and sparkling and absolutely empty.

But old BERNARD *and* JEAN *act exactly as though everything is perfectly normal. They settle themselves at a little table.*

There is no music.

JEAN: (*Bright-eyed*) Oh, it's nice! Isn't it nice! Doesn't it bring everything back like it used to be!

BERNARD: How do you mean?

JEAN: When we were dancing here. All those years ago.

BERNARD: (*Heavy sigh*) Yes.

JEAN: Do you remember?
(*Pause.*)

BERNARD: Yes.

JEAN: What's the matter? What are you looking at?

BERNARD: That light.

JEAN: What light? (*Alarmed*) Bernard? What are you talking about? What light?

BERNARD: (*Angrily*) *That* light!
(*As at the end of scene 13, the lights are down, and a big pool of bright white spotlight is slithering slowly around the ballroom. It settles on the dance band, which is now there. And on the singer—* JACK BUTCHER.)

BUTCHER: (*Sings*) I'm not a poet
How well I know it
I've never been a raver
But when I speak of you
I rave a bit, it's true
I'm wild about you
I'm lost without you
You give my life its flavour
What sugar does for tea

185

That's what you do for me.
(*The spotlight slides around the great room, slithers along the empty dance floor, then settles on young* BERNARD *and* JEAN, *dancing alone in the middle of the polished floor. The* SINGER *now in darkness.*)
(*Off, sings*) You're the cream in my coffee
    You're the salt in my stew
    You will always be
    My necessity
    I'd be lost without you

    You're the starch in my collar
    You're the lace in my shoe
    You will always be
    My necessity
    I'd be lost without you!
(*The light slips gently off the young dancers and slides slowly to the edge of the dance floor where it settles in a dazzling white pool on old* BERNARD. *The music dies away. The spotlight goes off. Darkness. Sound of his breathing. Slowly the lights come up—and the sounds—of—*)

49. BALLROOM: 1979
Reality. A latter-day dinner dance. A rather punkish modern group slamming through their number.

    BERNARD'*s and* JEAN'*s table is by the side of the dance floor.* JEAN *has bright eyes. She is all but tapping out the tune with one hand on the table.*
JEAN: (*Eventually*) I'm glad we came, Bernard. For the first time I can honestly say I'm glad we came back here.
(*He doesn't answer. Music continues. People dancing.*)
(*Enthusiastically*) Brings it all back, doesn't it, Bernard?
(*He doesn't answer. She looks at him. Her face becomes anxious. She touches his arm.*)
Bernard? What's the matter, aren't you feeling well?
(*Pause.*)
(*Alarmed*) Bernard?
(*He turns his head slowly and looks at her.*)
BERNARD: What did you say?

186

JEAN: I said I'm glad now that we came. It's nice. Brings it all back, somehow. Doesn't it?

BERNARD: Yes. It does. It does.

(*Pause. Music coming to an end. He is staring at her now with hostility. Applause.* JEAN, *too, is clapping.* BERNARD, *at the same time, is slowly and menacingly (and, yes, rather comically) rolling up the stiff drink and cocktail hotel menu which has been standing on the table.*)

JEAN: That was *lovely*!

BERNARD: A wasp.

JEAN: (*Startled*) What? Where—?

BERNARD: On your shoulder.

(*She goes into instant panic, flapping hands.*)

JEAN: Get it off—aah—get it off!

BERNARD: (*Hiss*) Hold still!

JEAN: Bernard! Get it off!

(*And then, in a frenzy, as she shrieks and recoils, he starts to beat her around the head, like an uncontrolled madman. People nearby rush to restrain* BERNARD. *He collapses, heavily, his heart finally giving out. The figures, and* JEAN, *cluster around him.*)

50. GRAND HOTEL

Lights splashing out into the summer dark.

Bring up music (no vocal) 'You're the Cream in My Coffee'.

Still pulling away as music continues.

Out across the dark sea, glistening on the moonlight. Unchanging, indifferent, empty.

Printed in the United Kingdom
by Lightning Source UK Ltd.
114236UKS00001B/204